Advance Praise f

"From astronauts to actresses, politician̲... managed the remarkable feat of convin̲... of life to talk candidly about their relationship with ̲... stories are alternately inspiring, touching, but always revealing. And in the end, Decker's book will move you to reflect on how Dear Old Dad shaped your life as well."

—Dean Foust, *BusinessWeek Magazine*

"By lending insights into the fathers of the famous, Jon Decker's book reminds us that values—honesty, persistence, generosity, selflessness—are the most important gift that a child can receive from a dad. This is a wonderful book."

—Vic Roberts, *The Christian Science Monitor*

"Fatherhood is the greatest thing that can ever happen to a man. I am grateful to my wife and to God for its wonders and heartaches. I am grateful to Jon Decker for helping me understand them."

—Paul Farhi, *The Washington Post*

"Forget about Moms! Dads are the thing! Yes, we all know how important mothers are in any person's upbringing, but has anyone really explored just how significant fathers are in this process? Well, they have now. Jon Decker's singular new book shows us that fathers play a surprisingly vital role in the nurturing of some of the world's most high-profile figures. Give the book a read, it makes for some great stuff."

—Andy Serwer, *Fortune Magazine*

"Had anyone ever doubted how central fathers are in our lives, Jon Decker's collection of celebrity sons and daughters should convince them otherwise. Fathers are our heros, our role models, the men we measure all others against. There are many kinds of fathers here, but different as they are, they have all left indelible imprints and lessons in the lives of their children. Special moments glow in the retelling and love shines from the pages. This is a very special book."

—Helle Bering, *The Washington Times*

Dear Joe,
We are so excited for you - as you begin your family! We're so proud of you as you begin a new chapter.
With love & Prayers
Your Sister Maggie
family
Aug. 2008

Great Dads

A Celebration of Fatherhood

Jonathan P. Decker

Adams Media Corporation
Holbrook, Massachusetts

Dedication

To my mother, my sister, and my late grandmother—
three incredible women who raised me in the absence of a father.

Published by
Adams Media Corporation
260 Center Street, Holbrook, MA 02343. U.S.A.

ISBN: 1-58062-277-1

Printed in Canada.

J I H G F E D C B A

Library of Congress Cataloging-in-Publication Data
Great dads : a celebration of fatherhood /
edited by Jonathan Decker.
p.   cm
ISBN 1-58062-277-1
1. Fatherhood. 2. Fathers. I. Decker, Jonathan.
HQ756 .G66   2000
306.874'2--dc21   00-028868
CIP

Cover photo ©Andrew McKim/Masterfile

This book is available at quantity discounts for bulk purchases.
For information, call 1-800-872-5627.

Visit our Web site: www.adamsmedia.com

Introduction and Acknowledgments

The importance of a father/son or father/daughter relationship has often been overlooked by the media. Stories of abuse, neglect, and abandonment overshadow the hundreds of stories of love, inspiration, and nurturing that fathers provide their children. A dad provides guidance, instills a value system, and teaches by example. These lessons and words of wisdom last a lifetime and they are passed down to future generations. Perhaps there is a common thread to the success stories of so many famous men and women who have been lucky enough to have a father who is also their hero.

This is a book that tells these stories. Leaders (both men and women) from the fields of politics, business, sports, entertainment, and the arts and sciences have contributed their first-person accounts of the lessons they learned from their fathers. Their stories are enlightening, touching, and often inspirational. I hope that fathers and fathers-to-be will read them and appreciate their important role in raising a son or a daughter.

A rather large number of people have made this book possible, either directly by contributing to it or indirectly by providing guidance and support.

I especially appreciate the advice of Bill Schulz and Dan Levine of *Reader's Digest*. Besides editing and publishing a shorter version of this book for the magazine, they were both very helpful in shaping the tone of the stories and getting the ball rolling in writing this book. David Cay Johnston of the *New York Times* was the person who recognized that the *Reader's Digest* article would make a wonderful book and helped guide me through the writing process. David then introduced me to my literary agent, Joel Fishman of The Bedford Book Works, Inc. Joel believed in this project from the start and saw its commercial appeal. He also was a good friend who will always have a seat with me at the U.S. Open! Caroline Nielson proved to be a great sounding board for ideas and people to interview. She also went above and beyond the call of any girlfriend and helped me transcribe dozens of hours of interviews. My editor, Edward Walters of Adams Media Corporation, did a terrific job of putting this book together. I am also grateful to Dr. Barbara Hines and Dean Jannette

Dates of Howard University who gave me the support to complete this project—even in the dog days of the summer of '99!

I cannot thank my mother, Beverly Decker, my aunt, Lucille Merchant, and my sister, Miriam Greenberg, enough for all of their help. I also want to thank all of the public relations people for making this book possible. Special thanks go to Dick Guttman of Guttman Associates, Phil de Picciotto of Octagon, Alison Leslie and Ann Israel of Marleah Leslie and Associates, Joe Lynch of the ATP Tour, Lee Patterson of the PGA Tour, and John Griffin of NASCAR. Finally, nothing would have been possible without the cooperation of all of the celebrities who shared their stories of laughter, tears, and poignancy about their fathers with me. To all of them, I am eternally grateful.

—J.P.D.
January 2000

Contents

James Woods

Actor

I WAS AN ARMY BRAT, WHICH MEANT
that I grew up all over the place.
I lived in Guam, Wisconsin,
Illinois, Virginia, Utah, and
Colorado—until we finally settled
in Rhode Island.

Despite my father's military
background, he was the opposite
of strict. To those he loved, he
was very kind and tender. He was
also extremely modest about his
achievements. He won two
Purple Hearts and a presidential
citation for bravery. He was a
great war hero, yet he never
talked about what he had
experienced.

Dad was a child of the
depression, as was my mom.
Consequently, they were very
concerned that their children
have the things that they never
had. What was amazing about my

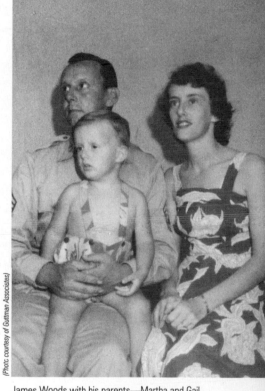

(Photo courtesy of Guttman Associates)

James Woods with his parents—Martha and Gail.

father was that he provided for us and protected us, even though he didn't
make that much money in the service. He always put our needs first.

When I was about 11 years old, I desperately wanted a record player
for Christmas. I loved rock 'n' roll, and all of my favorite songs were
coming out on forty-fives. But I also realized that on his salary, Dad
couldn't afford to buy me one. So in his spare time, he got a job in the
PX in the Armory. That Christmas he worked one hour a day during

lunch for 25 days at $1 an hour. He swallowed his pride and waited on guys that were his subordinates just to buy me that record player.

A year later, my father needed heart surgery and had a section of his aorta replaced. It was one of the first operations of its kind. He was on the operating table for 17 hours and had to undergo 21 blood transfusions. One of the transfusions didn't match properly and as a result, he had a transfusion reaction. Gradually, one by one, his organs broke down. For five days he knew he was dying.

On his last day he phoned my three-year-old brother to tell him that he had died and gone to heaven. He said, "God let me make a phone call to say good-bye to you. So don't be afraid and don't worry because I am fine. I just wanted you to know that I am thinking of you."

To me, he wrote a letter. In it, he told me how proud he was of me and my accomplishments in school. He expressed his hope that I would go to M.I.T. someday—which I eventually did. And he told me that he was certain that I would succeed in whatever I strived for. Mom handed me this letter on the day I was being honored with some other kids at an honors dinner for seventh and eighth graders. It was a big day for me. What I didn't realize was that as he wrote this letter, he knew he had little time left. When he died in my mother's arms, the last thing he said to her was, "Make sure that Jimmy gets to that dinner and don't tell him about this until after it's over." He wanted to make sure that I enjoyed this ceremony and didn't want to ruin a very special moment for me. He was a truly brave and decent man. He was a hero to me in his everyday life.

There's a myth that if you lose a parent, it's okay and you can get beyond it. It isn't. It is the most devastating thing that can happen to a child. But that said, he gave me values that have never once failed me. He taught me to always give respect to others and to demand it in return. He taught me to be kind to others and demand it of them. And he taught me to believe in myself and always try to be my very best.

My mom and dad had only one really serious argument—and it involved money. He wanted to get mortgage insurance on our house.

He told her, "It's the one investment we have and if anything ever happens to me, you and the kids can keep the house."

"We can't afford it," she said. "It's $14.75 a month."

Six months after this argument, Dad passed away and my mom thought we'd have to leave the house. But about three weeks later, a man came by and knocked on our door. It was a guy from the insurance company with a check for the entire payment on the house. My father had somehow scraped the money together for mortgage insurance and paid for it himself. Even from the grave, he was helping. He was without a doubt the most remarkable man I have ever known. I was absolutely blessed to have had such a wonderful dad.

◆ James Woods is a Golden Globe and Emmy Award winning film and television actor.

Joyce Brothers, Ph.D.

Psychologist, Syndicated Columnist

MY FATHER WAS AN ATTORNEY WHO HANDLED JUST ABOUT ANYTHING THAT walked in the office. He didn't specialize in anything. Instead, he was like today's general practitioner—he handled everything. While many lawyers often look for all the downsides and all the negatives in a situation, Dad's attitude about life and about law was, "Let's see how we can make this fair and make it happen." He was the kind of lawyer who made things work. I learned that attitude from him. If you make a fair, win-win deal, then it lasts a lifetime.

One of the things I learned from my dad is that a male chauvinist can be reconstructed. He married a woman who he said was his right hand, and they practiced law together their entire lives. But over the years he realized that she was not his right hand. She was his equal. Consequently, we learned that men and women could have equality long before we knew anything about women's liberation. That served as encouragement for my sister and me to become professional women.

My dad was a wonderful father who was always there for us. We never realized that we didn't have much money in the family because the things we did were so much fun. Dad took us to all types of museums in New York City and when we took vacations, we would usually stay at an inexpensive bed and breakfast. When it rained, we would even have picnics in the living room! We had no idea that all these adventures were calculated to be inexpensive. And we never knew until my father died that we had limited funds.

When mother and father would come home from work, we would always have dinner together. The conversation at dinner was led by my father and it dealt with what was happening in the world. He pressed my sister and me to give opinions and to fight for our point of view. I remember thinking how extraordinary it was for a man to care about what two little girls think.

One news story that my father and I had differing views on was President Roosevelt's attempt to pack the Supreme Court. There was nothing in concrete that said there could only be nine justices. So FDR tried to pack the Court in order to have decisions more favorable to the things he was trying to do for the country. Both Mom and Dad wanted to see all the reforms occur. But I thought that this was wrong and I fought for my point of view over the dinner table.

When President Roosevelt lost in his attempt to increase the number of Supreme Court justices, Dad came home with a surprise. He took out a big bottle of apple juice and champagne glasses and toasted the fact that I stayed with my opinion and fought for what I believed in. He was extremely proud. It was much harder to get praise from my dad than it was from my mother. He was the much more stern taskmaster. But, when you got it, it was terribly meaningful.

Dad gave me the confidence to believe in myself. It was the kind of confidence that allowed us to tackle much larger problems, and I think it was a very important factor in my becoming what I am today and my sister becoming a judge.

(Photo courtesy of Dr. Joyce Brothers)

Dr. Joyce Brothers

◆ Dr. Joyce Brothers is a monthly columnist for *Good Housekeeping*, a contributing editor for *Reader's Digest*, and has had her newspaper advice column syndicated through King Features for almost 30 years.

Jeff Bezos

Founder, Chairman, and CEO, Amazon.com

THE KEY VALUE MY FATHER INSTILLED IN ME GROWING UP WAS HARD WORK. His job with Exxon meant several moves throughout my childhood. I grew up mostly in Texas and then when I was about 12 we moved to Pensacola, Florida. After a few years there, we moved to Miami where I attended high school. In our family, work came before everything else. As a result, we always knew that our family vacations were subject to cancellation at the last second. Still, we managed to go on at least half of them! I admired my father's work ethic from a very early age. The people you admire are the people that you learn from, and I certainly have learned a ton from my dad.

My father came to the United States from Cuba alone when he was 15 years old. Fidel Castro was letting young people leave the island, but not adults, so his parents couldn't leave. When he came here, he knew only one word of English—"hamburger"—and that kept him alive for awhile. He then spent the first few weeks in America in a refugee camp in the Everglades and was taken on by a Catholic mission in Delaware. The mission ended up paying for his college education in Albuquerque and he's never forgotten that gesture or the blessings of this country.

My father is more American than anybody I know because he feels very passionate about the United States. In fact, we didn't speak Spanish at home because he wanted us to be completely American. Dad was genuinely appreciative of the freedoms and liberties that we have here.

Dad is a very disciplined person in his own life, but he's also very loving and warm. He also always did the right thing and taught by example. He felt that you can't just talk about right and wrong. Dad just did it and made sure I was paying attention.

My dad also made sure that I learned to be independent. From the age of four until my sophomore year in high school, he used to send me every summer to my maternal grandfather's ranch in Texas. I learned there what all ranchers know—self-reliance. That lesson is taught better in Southwest Texas because every day in the summer it's 107 degrees. You learn this lesson twice as fast in that kind of heat! The ranch was such a special place for me and I feel blessed to have had this experience. You learn different things from grandparents than you learn from parents, and I think my parents knew that.

The most important values I learned from my dad were hard work, self-reliance, and doing the right thing—even if it seems very painful in the short term. My dad believed that if he could get those sort of values instilled in us, we would have a much better than even chance of having a happy life.

(Photo courtesy of Amazon.com)

Jeff Bezos

My parents are very proud of me and my brother and sister. They have had a shrine to us in this one designated room in their house for as long as I can remember. It started out with drawings that we did as children and it has progressed to collections of business cards and press clippings.

When I told my dad of my plans for Amazon.com he was immediately supportive. He listened to my own ideas carefully and he also had suggestions. He thought the idea of selling books on the Internet was a great idea. But my dad really wasn't betting on the idea as much as he was betting on me. That is the kind of special relationship that a close family has.

I believe it would have been very difficult to go out on one of these weird paths—like Amazon.com certainly was five years ago—without that kind of support network. He is indeed a great dad and I am extremely proud of him.

◆ Jeff Bezos, the founder and CEO of Amazon.com, has helped foster the point-and-click revolution that is changing the way Americans shop. In 1999, he was named *Time* magazine's Person of the Year.

Derek Jeter

Shortstop, New York Yankees

MY DAD PLAYED BASEBALL IN COLLEGE AND WHEN I WAS YOUNGER, I WANTED to be just like him. It may sound corny, but when I was growing up, I thought my dad was cool. I looked up to him. He played baseball. He was very intelligent. He was probably my first role model.

My parents always stressed to my sister and me to get involved in different activities—whether it was athletics or extracurricular things in school. I played baseball, basketball, and soccer. I tried football but I was too skinny! But I just took a liking to baseball early on. Because I was born in New Jersey, I wanted to play for the New York Yankees.

Despite my love of baseball, education was first and foremost in our house. We couldn't play sports and we couldn't hang out unless we got good grades. Before every school year, my dad and mom required us to sign a handwritten contract that spelled out our expected grades, our chores, our curfew, and rules regarding drugs and alcohol. I never saw this contract as being negotiable. These were the rules my parents set and I had to live by them. Dad also stressed being honest and working hard. He always said, "Anything is possible if you work hard enough." He instilled confidence in me from a very early age.

As I continued to improve in baseball, my dad told me, "You can't compare yourself to who you're playing with or against in Kalamazoo. You have guys who are working just as hard all over America." He told me that if I wanted to succeed in achieving my dream of playing for the Yankees, I had to have more heart than the next guy. "Other players may be better," he said, "but there's no reason why someone should out-work you."

Baseball is a humbling sport in that it is a sport of failure. In this game you're going to fail more than you succeed. But my dad taught me that you've got to take the good with the bad and keep an even keel. You can't walk around with your head up high when you're doing well and then go hide in the corner when things go bad. You've got to try and have the same approach and same demeanor regardless of the situation. Dad always seems to be that way.

When we played against Cleveland recently, I was 0 for 5. I just had a terrible day. But in the game of baseball, you sometimes get a chance to redeem yourself. In the ninth inning, I got a hit to win the game. If this wasn't a great enough game, my dad was also at the ballpark to see me and the team come through in the clutch. As I came into the dugout to join in the celebration, I caught a glimpse of my dad in the stands. He was high-fiving everybody and acting like a fool!

I had my first full year in the big leagues in 1996, and I think my dad was real proud of how I handled

(Photo courtesy of the New York Yankees)

Derek Jeter

myself. I know he's happy that the Yankees have been successful. But I actually think he's more proud of how I've handled myself off the field. Dad's especially pleased that I started the Turn 2 Foundation, which works to steer high-risk kids away from drugs. In some ways I think this gives him a bigger thrill than my performance on the field. Two years ago, my dad—a drug and alcohol abuse counselor with a Ph.D.—gave up his practice to run the foundation. It makes me feel good to work with him on something so meaningful.

Whether it was academics or athletics, my parents were always the first ones to say how proud they were of me and my accomplishments. As long as I can remember, my dad let me know that he would support me no matter what. He made it clear to me from an early age that he was going to love me whether I got three hits or none. But he also will be the first one to tell me when I'm doing something wrong. I respect him and his judgment.

My dad is my best friend. I go to him for his advice and for his opinions and I know he's going to be honest with me. I trust him.

Dad treats everyone with respect and treats them the way he would want to be treated. It makes no difference whether he knows you or not, everyone just loves my dad. He's a special person.

◆ Derek Jeter is the all-star shortstop for the New York Yankees, the 1999 World Series Champions.

Al Gore

Vice President, 2000 Presidential Candidate

ALTHOUGH MY FATHER STARTED OUT A SCHOOL TEACHER, FROM THE TIME I was born he was always involved in public service. He instilled in me from an early age a belief in fighting for principle, and fighting for those who don't have a powerful voice in our society. He also taught me the importance of being a good dad—spending time with your kids, and being their first teacher.

As a parent, there are always conflicts between work and parenting. And that conflict, I've found, rises to an even higher level when you hold public office.

Throughout my public life, I've always put school and family events on my schedule before anything else. Two years ago, I was at one of my daughter's soccer games while Tipper was out of town making a speech on mental health. I had arranged my schedule to accommodate the game, and also a meeting with a head of state from a pretty fair-sized country later that afternoon. I figured that I would watch the game, congratulate my daughter, and then head back to the White House for this bilateral meeting. What I didn't count on was how competitive this game would get. The soccer match ended up going into overtime. I looked at my watch and began to get a little bit concerned about the time. But I figured, "no big deal." Then the game went into double overtime—and there was a pretty long delay between the two overtime periods! (And it was my turn to give out the snacks after the game!) So I just decided that the game was ultimately more important.

I ended up arriving for the meeting 45 minutes late, and I gave the interpreter a real workout in explaining my tardiness to this head of state. But as it turned out, he had young kids too, and it certainly broke the ice. We somehow avoided a major diplomatic incident! I've always tried to take the same approach with my children that my father took with me. He, of course, had important responsibilities in the Senate, but he never neglected his duties as a father. He was always there for us.

My father never pressured me to enter politics. In fact, he left it totally up to me. When I called him to tell him that I decided to run for Congress, he actually almost discouraged it. He said, "It's a long, hard road." He then went out of his way to tell me all the reasons not to do it. None of these arguments dissuaded me. I vowed to make the run for a Congressional seat and to do it completely on my own. I told my father that I didn't want him to make any speeches for me, or write any letters to supporters. He chafed at that idea. Like any father, he wanted to help me in any way he could. But he knew that proving myself and establishing my independence was important, and he agreed to stay behind the scenes. I'll never forget the look on his face on election night. He was beaming. He was so happy and proud of what I had accomplished.

I also learned a tremendous amount about courage from my father. He embodied what public service is all about. One of the most important votes my father ever cast was in his last term in the Senate. The Voting Rights Act of 1965 was one of those bills that posed a difficult choice for Southern lawmakers. But for my father, doing the right thing was never a difficult choice. He refused to sign the Southern Manifesto in the 1950s—

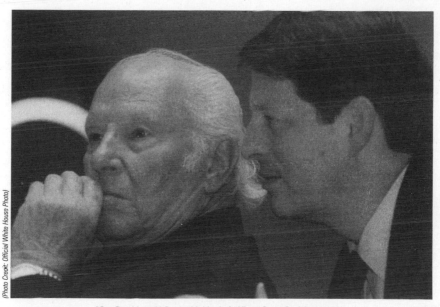

(Photo Credit: Official White House Photo)

Vice President Al Gore with his dad, Albert Gore, Sr. (circa 1993).

a statement opposing integration—after the Supreme Court's Brown vs. The Board of Education decision. He also supported the Civil Rights Act of 1957. But in 1965, the storm clouds were gathering and the country was in the midst of controversy over the Vietnam War. My father was a leading opponent of the war and was always a leading civil rights advocate. He not only voted for the Voting Rights Act, he also decided to oppose President Nixon's nominees to the Supreme Court, because of his concern that they would not support civil rights. Our whole family saw pretty clearly the burden he was going to carry into his next re-election campaign. But he made it very clear that it was important to do the right thing, to stand on principle, and to fight the good fight. I am immensely proud of him and the courage that he demonstrated. When a father shows courage in support of the right principles, children learn some of the most powerful lessons they can ever be taught. My father was both a role model and a hero to me.

◆ Albert Gore, Jr. is the Vice President of the United States. He has secured the 2000 Democratic nomination for President.

Sammy Sosa

Outfielder, Chicago Cubs

I GREW UP WITH MY FOUR BROTHERS and two sisters in the Dominican Republic and I'm very proud to be from there. I come from a very solid family where hard work was stressed above everything else. I was only seven years old when my father passed away. But in the short amount of time that we spent together, he raised me the right way. I always knew he loved me very much. He would take me everywhere, even to work. He had a small business—a tractor from which he sold fruits and vegetables in town. He worked there every day from sun up until sun down.

(Photo Credit Stephen Green, 1998, courtesy of the Chicago Cubs)

Sammy Sosa

Despite all of his hard work, we struggled very much to make ends meet. It was tough, and it got even more difficult when my dad passed away. When that happened, my mother did everything that she could with the business to provide for us. Even though I was a small boy, I also worked to try and make money for my family. I learned to be a man earlier than most of my friends. I never had the opportunity to play with other kids my age as I was too busy working for my mom.

I wish my father were alive today so that he could enjoy everything that God has given to me. I think about this sometimes when special things happen in my life. He was in my thoughts very often over the past two magical years and I would have loved so much to have shared my accomplishments with him.

Another regret that I have is that I never got a chance to have a catch with my father. I didn't start playing baseball until I was 14. My brother Luis was the one who played, and he introduced me to the game. He saw my talent and got me involved in little league.

Today, I have two boys and two girls and my beautiful wife, Sonia. I teach my kids everything. I teach them right from wrong like my father did. I also teach them honesty and hard work—the same values I learned from watching my father work every day. I appreciate every moment with my wife and my four children. We spend so much time together—not only during the season in Chicago, but also during the off-season back in the Dominican Republic. The sense of loss that I experienced with my father is something I never want them to know.

◆ Sammy Sosa is the all-star center fielder for the Chicago Cubs. In 1999, he became the first player in major league history to hit more than 60 home runs in consecutive seasons.

Katharine Graham

Chairman of the Executive Committee, The Washington Post Company

I GREW UP IN WASHINGTON. MY FATHER WORKED FOR THE WAR FINANCE Corporation during and after World War I. In the '20s, he worked for the Farm Loan Board, and under President Hoover he was governor of the Federal Reserve Board. When President Roosevelt came in to office, my father stepped down because he didn't agree with the president's monetary policies. Just three weeks later, his life changed forever. The *Washington Post* became available. It was a once-in-a-lifetime opportunity and he didn't waste any time buying it at a bankruptcy auction on the steps of the building.

Growing up, my father was very distant because he was extremely busy with his government service. It wasn't until I got older—in late high school and college—that we grew much closer. We were then able to talk to each other as adults. During my college years, he was the dominant figure in my life in terms of providing guidance and advice. He made me feel that he believed in me, and this instilled in me a great sense of confidence.

My father would write to me at college and fill me in on news about the *Post*. All of my letters from him were full of things about the paper and the progress that he was making. Our relationship had developed into one that was very grown up and trusting. We had become incredibly close.

Dad had a great sense of humor and could be very funny. My sister once sent him a telegram from Vassar saying, "Allowance early or bust!" He immediately sent her back a telegram that read, "Bust!"

I loved newspapers even before my father bought the *Post*. I worked on my high school newspaper and always thought I'd go into journalism. When I graduated from college, my father said to me, "I'm heading out to a retreat at the Bohemian Grove. Why don't you come ride out on the train with me to San Francisco? We can talk. I haven't seen you in such a long time." I took him up on his invitation. It sounded fun, and I had never been to California. After spending a few days in San Francisco, I said to my father, "I love this town and will swallow my pride if you'll help me get a job here." Within a few days I was working for the *San Francisco News*.

My first week on the job he was still in California visiting his sister. One day I came home in tears. I didn't know how to type. I didn't know the city. I didn't know anything.

"I've bitten off more than I can chew. I can't do this," I told my father. "I'm coming home with you."

Rather than letting me give up so easily, he said, "Why don't you try it a little longer? It won't hurt. And then you can give it up anytime you want to." I tried it for another week or two and began to love it.

When my father came back out to California in the spring, he said to me, "You always said you would come home to work, and I hope you will." It seemed like a good time, and I agreed.

Dad let me establish my independence at the paper. I would see him occasionally at work and he treated me no differently from any other employee. Initially, I worked in the editorial department and then moved on to the Sunday section. He had very high standards—especially for

(Photo courtesy of Katharine Graham)

Katharine Graham with her father, Eugene Meyer.

me—but he was also the type of person to praise me when he saw my work.

My father ran the paper with great integrity. He was a Republican, but when he bought the *Post*, he said, "This paper is not going to be a mirror of the publisher's interests. It's not going to be Republican. It's going to be independent. It's going to report the news as it sees it." And that's the way it stayed. I think that was so large of him because a lot of newspapers in those days reflected the views of the publisher, but my father would never have that.

I think he would be absolutely thrilled with how far the *Post* has come since 1933. He had a hard time when he started because he wasn't a newspaperman and he made a lot of mistakes. It was uphill all the way, and he really got discouraged at times, but he worked terribly hard to make it better and more profitable. The marvelous thing my father did was to increase the circulation, the advertising, and the quality every year. I think that people these days—because of the high profile we got through the Pentagon Papers and Watergate—forget the enormous role my father played in building this paper.

My dad was certainly a mentor. I was immensely attached to and fond of him—and I still am. I look back on what he did for me with extreme gratitude.

◆ Katharine Graham is the chairman of the Executive Committee of the Washington Post Company.

George W. Bush

Governor of Texas, 2000 Presidential Candidate

WHEN I WAS TWO, WE MOVED FROM NEW HAVEN—WHERE DAD HAD JUST graduated from college—to Midland, a very remote town in West Texas. My first memories of my dad were related to sports. Baseball was my favorite sport growing up and I suspect it was because he and I played catch all the time. I remember the first time he said, "Son, I feel comfortable throwing it as hard as I can to you." It was a very proud moment.

One of the lessons I can clearly remember learning from my dad was to "respect your elders." I can remember at times being admonished for not being as polite to older people as I should have been. I also remember lessons of "Don't lie, cheat, or steal." These were basic values, but Dad and Mother set some very high standards. If you slipped up, they let you know.

One of the things Dad never tried to do, though, was to dictate to me what I should do with my life. He never tried to put his blueprint for my life over mine. His attitude was, "I'm going to teach you basic values. I'm going to unconditionally love you. And I'm going to expect you to chart your own way in life." My father knew that he could unduly influence me and all his kids. He could tell that we all loved him so much.

I think the greatest gift a parent can give is unconditional love. A father should say to his child, "I love you. No matter what you do, I love you." Of course you expect your child not to do bad things, but I think you need to instill in your child the idea that he or she will be loved their whole life. Dad did this with me and he did it with my brothers and sister.

I've seen my dad go through some tough times. I was old enough to remember when my sister died. He was very brave about the loss of his daughter. I also saw him lose more than once in the political process. Three times—two Senate races and a presidency. He didn't like to lose and he was clearly disappointed. But he was strong and gracious in defeat and he never passed on blame to anybody else. Instead, he accepted his fate in a very noble way. My father is a very strong man and a very good man.

I think one of the most important lessons I've learned from him is not to fear failure. I don't fear failure because I've got the most important ingredients in life at hand—my family and my faith. I also don't fear success.

I learned the lesson about not fearing failure from my dad because I've seen him fail and know what a great man he is. Losing a campaign does not mean losing your integrity or losing your decency or losing his standing in my eyes or in the eyes of honorable people. I think that's an important lesson for anybody in life to have to learn. We must take risks in order to succeed and if it doesn't work out for the moment, life itself will work out in the long run.

(Photo Credit: George Bush Presidential Library)

George W. Bush with his dad, George.

This is a lesson that's hard to absorb until you're ready to absorb it. It's hard for a young man to observe until he's observant. And as a teenager—like most teenagers—I wasn't very observant. These lessons that my father taught me really became a part of my being as I got older.

My dad is a World War II veteran. He and his generation strongly believed in the concept of "duty, honor, and country." That sums up much of his life. He has always felt that one has a duty to serve one's country in an honorable way. It's not surprising that he feels very strongly about that—not only because of the lessons he learned from his dad, but because that was the motto of a generation of young men and women who went to fight in World War II.

I obviously have inherited from him this same sense. I became interested in politics and the political process because of him. I ran for Congress in 1978 and lost. I came in second in a two-man race! It was a tough campaign and I lost to a good man who ran a very good campaign. But after making a living in the private sector for 18 years, I got back into politics.

I suspect that had I not been raised by a man who came into the political process with his integrity and left with his integrity, that I would have been discouraged about getting back into politics in the first place. His presence in the political arena—the fact that he achieved a lot, the fact that he found the process to be invigorating, and the fact that he exited with his integrity—sent strong signals to both me and my brother Jeb. I think it's a great tribute to my dad that two sons ran for office shortly after he left office. It's a great testimony to two wonderful parents.

My last name has opened up some doors. I also think it has shut some. I have inherited half of my father's friends and all of his enemies! I have had to work hard in Texas to pick up the other half of his friends and peel off some of his enemies.

Still, I think it's been an easy name to live up to because he carried it so well. It's not an embarrassment to be George Bush's son. I have a great sense of pride. I developed a reputation in my father's 1992 presidential campaign of being fiercely loyal. And I was. I was a warrior on his behalf because I think he's the greatest dad that's ever walked. I can't imagine having a better father. He is the most humble and considerate person I think I've ever met. It's been easy for me to carry the name. When people ask, "You're George Bush's son?" I say, "You bet I am. And proud of it," without any hesitation.

In terms of opening doors, obviously in the political process, there's only one person who can open a door and that's the candidate. You can knock on that door and somebody's going to say either, "Come on in," or "Sorry, not interested in having you." My father taught me that you've got to go out and earn people's respect and earn people's votes. In this line of work, you've got to prove yourself.

Now that I'm a father, I'm trying to teach my daughters what my father taught me at an early age: "You're responsible for your actions and decisions." You can't blame somebody else if something goes bad. I think that's one of the really important lessons our culture needs to learn as well.

Above all, I learned this from my father: Being a dad is the most important job I'll ever have.

◆ Bush is the governor of Texas and a former owner of the Texas Rangers baseball club. He has secured the 2000 Republican nomination for President.

Lani Guinier

Professor, Harvard Law School

WHAT I REMEMBER MOST ABOUT MY father was the way he celebrated my accomplishments. He was always so invested in my life—without ever being controlling. Dad gave me enormous freedom to pursue my own passions. But he always made it clear that he wanted me to go to Harvard and graduate—because he never got that chance.

My father was admitted to Harvard in 1929 but he had to drop out two years later because Harvard refused to give him any financial aid. It was ostensibly on the grounds that he had failed to submit a picture with his application.

(Photo courtesy of Lani Guinier).

Lani Guinier and her dad, Ewart Guinier.

But it was always his understanding that they discovered after admitting him that he was black. Dad went on to graduate from City College in New York and then received a Masters from Columbia and ultimately a law degree from NYU.

The day I received my acceptance letter from Harvard is a day I'll never forget. My father actually came down to my high school cafeteria during lunch and handed me the envelope. I was a little embarrassed that my father would show up like this. But it was also a source of joy that he cared that much. It tickled me. He never said, "You have to do this." But the message that I got from my father was, "I am so proud that you have this option." My father wanted me to have a different experience than he did. He wanted me to have a better life.

The number one value my father instilled in me was to fight injustice. He taught me to fight for what's right and not to accept anything less. He also taught me to be a person of principle and to believe in something that's bigger than myself. Dad's lessons came from his own experiences.

In the late 1940s, my father testified about redistricting before a Senate committee. Because of his color, he couldn't stay in any hotels near the Capitol and he couldn't eat in the Senate's public cafeteria. As he read his statement, one of the senators interrupted him and said, "You've got to lower your voice. You're speaking too loudly."

My father replied, "[If] I may seem to be a bit moved about this, it is because I am a Negro . . . I think Negroes are full-fledged American citizens and should have all the rights of American citizens and should have it today." Whereas many people would be extremely intimidated by this congressional panel, my father was bold and forthright. He was never afraid of speaking out for what he believed in.

Dad ultimately became a professor at Harvard. In fact, he was appointed to his position in my junior year. That year, my father used to take me out to dinner quite a bit. It was wonderful because we could share with each other our respective experiences. I talked to him about political questions that were being raised by my classmates on campus. And he was quite open with me about his own experiences coming back to Harvard. He was always very insightful.

My father was outraged by racism, but he was never bitter. He saw bitterness as a type of anger that is very unhealthy and counterproductive. He was passionate and forward thinking. He hoped that the injustices that he experienced would not be suffered by anyone else.

My most public disappointment occurred in 1993—three years after my father died. My nomination to lead the Justice Department's Civil Rights Division was never sent to the Senate. But in many ways, my Senate confirmation "nonexperience" was a moment of reconnection. I was able to summon my father's voice in my mind and benefit from his wisdom even though he wasn't present. I knew that he would have wanted me to stand on principle and fight for what I believed in. It was really with my father's permission and conviction that I could do that.

I learned from my father not to wallow in disappointment. He taught me to use these experiences to fight back—not only for myself, but also in a way that's constructive and beneficial to many others. He was a very generous person and despite his lifetime of disappointments, he was an incredible optimist.

◆ Lani Guinier, a third-generation attorney, is a tenured professor at Harvard Law School.

Larry King

Host, CNN's *Larry King Live*

MY DAD, WHOSE NAME WAS EDDY, came to the U.S. from Russia in 1918 when he was 18 years old. He loved America from the day he set foot on Ellis Island. In fact, he was so patriotic that when World War II broke out, he immediately tried to enlist. But he had just turned 40 and they didn't take anyone over 40.

I was very close to my dad. He had lost a son the year before I was born, so there was a special bond that we had for each other. What also made my childhood wonderful was the fact that I grew up in a loving household. I always knew that my dad and mom loved one another because they were always so affectionate. They were huggers and grabbers and kissers. Jews tend to be! On those rare occasions when they did disagree, they spoke in Yiddish. That was so my younger brother and I wouldn't understand!

Larry King. 1997 CNN, Inc. A Time Warner Co.

(Photo Credit: A. Eccles. Courtesy of "Larry King Live")

One of the values that my father instilled in me was truthfulness. I was supposed to go to Hebrew School every day after regular school. One day I decided not to go. I just wanted to play with my friends. Well, Dad found out about my playing hooky when he was coming home from work. He saw a friend of mine and asked how Hebrew School went and my friend mentioned that I wasn't there. Later at the dinner table he just calmly said, "How was Hebrew School today?" I said, "Fine." And before I knew what hit me, I was flying across the room. Dad had whacked me with the back of his hand. He never stopped eating his soup. My mom ran over to me. But Dad just looked over at me and in a booming voice he said, "Never lie." In a very real sense, he taught me lessons about honesty.

June 9, 1943, is a day I will never forget. It was a Saturday morning and I was coming home from the library. I was only about nine and a half at the time. As I got to the apartment building where we lived, I saw three squad cars parked in front. I immediately knew something was wrong. I ran to the house and the books I had checked out of the library went flying. I then heard my mother scream. As I got to the apartment lobby, an officer came downstairs, picked me up, put me in the squad car and we drove around for the day. He was the one who told me my father had died. He was only 43 when he collapsed on a bus going from Penn Station to his job at a defense plant in Carney, New Jersey.

For some reason I was angry at my father. I didn't understand death. I didn't understand his leaving. I didn't even go to the funeral. I just remember being hurt and disappointed.

When you grow up without a father at that age, it's a very difficult thing. The importance of a father is immense. Growing up, I missed this. I was envious of all my friends who had one. I was always the "fatherless boy" in my neighborhood.

When I had my first child, I think I subconsciously decided to be a very hands-on father. I was attentive and there for them. And although there came a time when I wasn't living with my kids, I always wanted them to know that I was supportive of them. Even though marriage didn't always work for me, fatherhood always did. I really valued the importance of the place a father has in a home. There's nothing like a happy marriage, but just because a marriage doesn't work out doesn't mean that you can't be a good dad. In fact, you should be a better dad. You should be much more aware of your responsibilities.

Of all the great things that have happened to me, the best thing I did was to be a father. I'm aware of fatherhood. I'm aware of the importance of the need to be there. Maybe I'm more aware of it because I lost my father. He was a very dominant and powerful figure in my life.

◆ Larry King is the Emmy Award–winning host of CNN's *Larry King Live*, which celebrates its 15th anniversary this year.

Alan "Ace" Greenberg

Chairman, Bear, Stearns & Co., Inc.

MY FATHER HAD MORE COMMON sense than anybody I have ever run into. His name was Ted Greenberg and he was my role model.

We grew up in Oklahoma City where Dad owned a chain of ladies' retail stores. He was always very concerned about the people he worked with and very considerate towards his customers. If anyone ever wanted to open a charge account, his employees had a standing order: "Don't ask them a lot of questions. Just open it up." Dad explained to me when I was a teenager his reason for this policy.

"If they buy something and don't pay, they can only beat me once," he said. "But if you make it easy to open a charge account, they'll remember you forever."

Quite frankly, he was that way with minority groups also. And getting a charge account for a minority in Oklahoma City in those days wasn't easy. But Dad's standing order applied to everyone.

(Photo courtesy of Alan Greenberg)

Alan "Ace" Greenberg with his dad, Ted.

"Don't ask them any questions," he'd say. "Just open the account and make them feel terrific."

During World War II, I saw a lot of people had cash. I didn't understand how this was possible with price controls in place. So I asked my father, "Where do these people get the cash and why don't we have a lot of cash?"

He said, "Well they do business off their books and they don't report it to the government."

"Why don't you?" I asked. And I'll never forget his reply.

"If I ever did something dishonest, I wouldn't be able to sleep at night," he said. "Plus, I don't ever want to end up working for my secretary or my accountant!" What Dad meant was if somebody knows you're stealing from Uncle Sam, those people are liable to blackmail you.

I realized when I was very young how smart he was and my brother, sister, and I all had a great deal of respect for him. We wanted to behave because we didn't like the consequences. There was never a question of smoking pot or drinking. That was out of the question. We just didn't do it.

Dad had a great sense of humor and he'd love to kid around with us. I remember when my brother was 16 how much he depended on borrowing my father's car to get around. One Saturday night at dinner, Dad noticed that my brother was very nicely dressed and it was obvious he had some plans.

My father said, "What are you going to do tonight?"

"I have a date," he said. "But I don't think you know her."

"I may not know her," Dad replied. "But I hope her dad has a nice big car!"

I have two grown children and I have tried to pass on to them those same values that my father instilled in me. As they grew up, they too appreciated their grandfather's sense of humor. But I think they were too young to realize just how brilliant he was.

◆ Alan "Ace" Greenberg is the chairman of Bear, Stearns & Co., Inc., the investment firm he joined in 1949.

Jesse Ventura

Governor of Minnesota

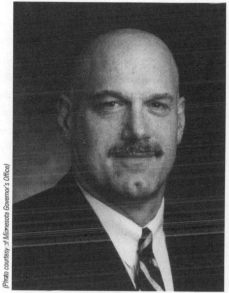

(Photo courtesy of Minnesota Governor's Office)

Governor Jesse Ventura

MY FATHER WAS A LABORER FOR the City of Minneapolis Street Department. He and my mom usually went off to work before I left for school and I got home before they did. Because my older brother and I were latch-key kids, we were taught early on to be very independent and to know how to take care of ourselves. Despite this independence, we never felt neglected in any way.

When I was growing up, the Beatles came into popularity and all of a sudden we all wanted long hair to our shoulders. My mom, though, didn't go for any of that. She would send me to the barber and I'd fight her tooth and nail. She would then appeal to my father.

"Make Jim go to the barber," she said. "He looks terrible."

My old man had an entirely different take on my new look. "What the hell do I care?" he said. "If he wants to have his hair down to his ass, that's his business. The only thing I ask of him is if we meet on the street, just pretend he doesn't know me." That was his attitude. He thought that hair doesn't make the person. He felt, "If he wants to look like an idiot, that's up to him." He was never judgmental about people. He just had this "live and let live" attitude.

I didn't wrestle in high school. I played football and swam. Dad would come out and watch me compete in the really big events—like the Twin

City Championships. But he wasn't one of those fathers that stood on the sidelines and lived vicariously through his son. Instead, he would generally stay at home for my games and then I would come home and tell him what happened. I always knew he cared.

My father was very political at the dinner table. In fact there were times when my mom would almost send him away from the table because he'd get so riled up watching the politicians on television! I think like any father, he didn't mind that his kids went into the service, being that he had gone through World War II. However, I think if he had his choice, he would have preferred us not going into the military. He knew enough about war because he had seven bronze battle stars from World War II. But because he raised us to be so independent, he knew that we had to follow our own life's course. He would never step in the way of decisions that we had to make. His only advice to me was, "If you're going to join the service, join the Air Force or the Navy. The Army won't teach you anything. At least in the Navy or the Air Force, they'll teach you something you can use later. Besides, the Army picks the shittiest places in the world and puts bases there." He even made it more explicit than that!

When Christmas came around, he would never buy presents. Instead, he always gave "green," which I liked better. We would open Christmas presents from other relatives and then at a certain point in time, Dad would pull out the wallet. He would peel off $200 and pass it around. Mom used to get angry at him because he wouldn't go shopping. But Dad would say, "This way they can buy what they want." Of course I would always be "shushing" my mom. I told her, "I like his presents . . . a lot of green presents!"

Even when I'd come home from leave when I was in the military, Dad would come sidle over to me and say, "Do you need a few bucks?" He was just so giving.

Dad was so popular and friendly that when I went into the military at age 18, my 18- and 19-year-old friends would still drive up to our lake cabin with a case of beer to play cards with my dad. I was off on my SEAL training and these guys would still want to hang around Dad at the cabin at least three times a summer. My father was 60 at this point and retired. He wasn't a surrogate grandfather or even a surrogate father to my buddies. He was just their friend.

What I learned from my father was to be a straight shooter. With my father, what you saw is what you got. He might say something that would offend people, but he would never do it intentionally. He just said what he believed and was never shy about speaking his mind if he felt something. For example, my father used to refer to President Nixon as "the tail-less rat" and Hubert Humphrey as "old rubber lip." He had a name for everything.

Today I am the chief executive officer of the state of Minnesota. I run the state that my dad raised me in. My dad would have never believed it. And if my father's looking down now, he's still not believing it!

◆ Jesse Ventura is serving his first term as the governor of Minnesota.

Cokie Roberts

Senior Political Correspondent, ABC News

ALL OF MY CONSCIOUS LIFE, MY FATHER WAS INVOLVED IN POLITICS. BECAUSE my parents understood they would be raising a family in politics, they made a determined decision to involve us in everything they did. And my brother and sister and I were thrilled with that!

When we were little children, we spent half the school year in Louisiana and half the school year in Washington. We divided our lives to accommodate the congressional schedule, until my brother went to the equivalent of junior high school. So we made a lot of adjustments in order to be together. And although my father was away a lot, I have a sense of him always being there for me. I learned from my parents that very busy people must and can carve out time for their families. He had incredible demands on him, but he somehow managed to be a terrific father.

Our house was always the place to be in Washington—especially for the members who were here without their families. Senators or congressmen were over at the house for dinner all the time. And one of the things that my mother and father were so incredible about was how they just completely included us in everything. It never occurred to my mom or dad that there was anything odd about us joining in a political argument with the Speaker of the House or the secretary of defense. It was just the way it was in our family.

My father always took us seriously. Even when we were children, our opinions mattered. We had many a raucous conversation at the dinner table and although we often disagreed, our opinions were always sought and valued. I think that for girls in particular, that is a very important thing for a father to do. It instilled in us a great amount of confidence and I think we all matured a lot faster as a result.

We would miss school regularly to go watch congressional debates. Daddy felt that was more important than coursework. His work and the work of Congress were affecting the world and we better know about it!

I still remember how excited I was on my seventh birthday. I was then old enough to go into the public gallery and take people on tours around the Capitol. That is what I looked forward to! I lived the political life and lived it happily.

Daddy could be very intimidating when he wanted to be. When my husband, Steve, got up the nerve to ask my father for my hand, Daddy's reaction was totally typical. It was a Sunday morning and my father knew that something was up. Rather than hang around the living room, Daddy escaped to his vegetable garden in the backyard. His solitude back there didn't last long; Mamma and I pushed Steve out the back door. Steve then went through this prepared speech and at the end of it, my father's reaction caught him a bit off-guard.

Without looking up from his tomatoes, he simply said, "Fine."

(Photo Credit: Maggie Smith, Courtesy of Cokie Roberts)

Cokie Roberts and her dad, Hale Boggs.

Steve was still quite nervous and tried to keep the conversation going. On a momentous occasion such as this, he didn't think their talk should be over so soon.

He said, "I know that you think there are going to be problems—my being Jewish and Cokie being Catholic. Is there anything you want to talk to me about that?"

Daddy replied, "Oh, you're going to have problems. That's for sure. But nowhere near as many problems as I would have if I tried to tell Cokie who to marry!"

I grew up in another era. Girls were expected to grow up, get married, have children, and do good things in the community. But I also wanted to have a career and Daddy never discouraged it. In fact, when I was on television at the tender age of 21, my father loved it. He watched faithfully and was very proud of my early success.

The last time I saw my father was in 1972 when he and Hubert Humphrey traveled to California to do some fundraising for congressional Democrats. I lived in Los Angeles at the time and my kids were just turning two and four. I still remember how he spent that Sunday with them at the hotel swimming pool. He just had a wonderful time with them. He was so utterly devoted to his grandchildren.

I miss my father very much. His intellectual rigor, his devotion to his family, and his fundamental goodness certainly had an enormous impact on me. But for me, the hardest part has been that he never saw my children grow up.

◆ Cokie Roberts is the senior political correspondent for *ABC News* and serves as the co-host of *This Week*.

Val Ackerman

President, WNBA

I HAVE HAD A LIFELONG CONNECTION TO SPORTS LARGELY BECAUSE OF MY DAD. He played basketball, baseball, and soccer at what was then Trenton State College. And ultimately he became the athletic director at my high school. As a kid I spent many hours tagging along after my dad when he went to various high school games and meets. When I got to high school, I was basically a four-seasons athlete. I played field hockey in the fall, basketball in the winter, ran track in the spring, and swam for a local swim club in the summer.

It was a huge thrill for me when I would see my dad in a corner of the gym or on the sidelines of the hockey field. I remember thinking how cool that was. Dad would have been interested in my games even if he had been an accountant. But the fact that he was the athletic director made my competing so much more fun. During the course of the day, I would also pop by his office. Sometimes I'd just sit down and listen to him on the phone. I learned so much from being around him. In fact, for the longest time, I just assumed that I would become an athletic director too. I guess, in a way, I ended up following his lead.

People liked my dad. Wherever we went, he was warmly greeted. He got along very well with students, parents, and other members of the faculty. My dad was just such a pleasant person. Whenever I saw him at a game or around school, he always had a smile on his face. He seemed to enjoy his work so much—especially interacting with people. He had wonderful people skills. And he impressed upon me the importance of having good relationships with people and having a pleasant manner. I think this is critical in any job, but especially in mine where I am at the intersection of so many groups of people. I deal with players, agents, coaches, writers, sponsors, and networks as well as all the team and league front office people. There is a premium on positive people and having good people skills. I see that as being my dad's biggest influence.

Despite his gregarious nature, my dad was outwardly not a very emotional person. At my senior sports banquet in high school, I was honored with an award. Instead of getting down off the stage and taking my seat after receiving it, I stayed up there. Nobody knew what I was going to say. And I kind of didn't either. But somehow, I got through a speech about what a great job my dad had done as athletic director. He drew up the schedules. He kept the fields looking sharp. And he made sure the referees got to the games on time.

"My dad—Mr. Ackerman to most of you—has never received any credit for any of his hard work," I said. "There's no award for Most Dedicated Athletic Director, but if there was, my dad would be the unanimous choice."

I remember looking over at my dad when I was finished with this speech and he had broken down and cried. He was usually such a stoic person, so his reaction completely surprised me. This moment said so much about our relationship.

I was about six hours away from home when I attended college in Charlottesville. But Dad and Mom somehow managed to come to several

(Photo courtesy of Val Ackerman)

Val Ackerman with her family (including her dad, Randy).

games. I believe that was a great source of pride for him—that he had a child who was playing basketball at the Division I, intercollegiate level.

My father wasn't a cheerleader kind of a dad. His actions tended to speak a lot louder than his words. But I always knew he was right behind me. In my freshman year at Virginia in 1977, our team wasn't that good. We were playing against teams that were much more evolved. And I learned that the hard way. At a Christmas tournament in Chapel Hill that year, we got blown out. I don't think I ever felt as bad about a loss as I did that day. My dad was there and he saw my pain. Right after the game, he whisked me back to New Jersey for Christmas break. In a very quiet way, Dad was very understanding of how devastating a loss that particular game was. Even without saying a word, I knew he was there.

I also learned from my dad to have passion for what you do. My dad loved working with kids and he loved being in sports. I remember coming home from law school after final exams, which were very stressful. My mom picked me up at the airport and after dropping off my suitcase at home, I went over to see Dad at my old high school. When I walked into the gym, I saw him playing volleyball with a bunch of high school sophomores. He was having a ball. I immediately thought, "What am I doing? This guy's got the best job in the world." I decided then that I wanted to have a job where I was as in love with what I was doing as he was.

I think my dad was as happy as I was the day that I got my job at the NBA. It was a great thrill for him to see me get a job in a league he had followed from the time he was a kid and where we had both had so many happy memories together. We were both die-hard pro-basketball fans. He had an undying love for the Boston Celtics, which I inherited. Of course I had to be neutral when I came to work for the league! One of my regrets, though, is that he's not around to see what happened in the WNBA. That's a big disappointment.

My dad made my brother and me a priority in his life. He gave us everything we needed in order to equip us to be adults. He was a hero, a mentor, and a role model.

◆ Val Ackerman, formerly a top executive with the NBA, is now the president of the WNBA.

Jay Leno

Host, *The Tonight Show*

I ALWAYS WANTED TO DO SOMETHING THAT MADE MY DAD FEEL PROUD OF ME. That was a huge deal. Every piece of construction paper that I drew on went on the refrigerator. Every project I did at school went on display in the dining room or the living room. And consequently, every bad thing I did went on display in the dining room or the living room! My parents just paid a lot of attention to me.

If my dad ever felt I was being taken advantage of by someone, he would take it personally. He never stopped telling me, "Hey you just get in there and fight the good fight, son!" If there was ever a bad review of my act in the paper, he'd say, "I'm gonna get that fella on the phone!" It was no different than when he found out that I was actually working at The Improv *for free!* Boy was he mad! "What the hell is that?" he'd say. "He's making money off of you!"

Dad wasn't all talk. He fought the good fight too. I remember when my dad was about 63, he came home from work and complained about one particular union guy who would come by his insurance office and give him trouble. This union guy was about 35 years old and he would always yell at my dad. He was a pretty big guy who did a lot of unnecessary finger-pointing and hollering. He was a real jerk and my dad couldn't stand him. Finally, he had had enough. He announced at the dinner table, "I'm gonna teach him a lesson. I'm gonna fight that guy."

So, at the age of 63 he started training! He ran five miles a day, every day, for about three months. He was also working out with the speed bag. Finally, in December, the union guy comes back again and starts yelling at my dad and poking him in the stomach. My dad started to holler back, and then suddenly: BOOM! My dad gave him a combination and knocked the guy out. When the guy eventually got up, he ran out of the building and called the police.

At this point, my father casually went back to his desk, put on his big, thick eyeglasses, and put in both of the hearing aids he sometimes wore. When the Andover policeman returned, he saw my dad and asked the union guy, "Is this the guy that beat you up?!" The union guy nodded. Then the cop started laughing hysterically at him. This just infuriated the union guy, who turned and stormed out of the office. My dad and the cop just kept on laughing.

Dad was an insurance salesman for most of his life. It was the perfect fit for him. He was always very gregarious, a good people guy, and a great salesman. He was also very protective of me. He tried to isolate me from certain things. I never saw my dad drunk and I never heard him swear. When I was seven, I went to an insurance convention with my father and he made sure that I didn't see anything inappropriate. I remember walking by a hotel room full of insurance men who were clearly getting drunk and acting silly. Dad saw this as well. He immediately grabbed me by the arm and tried to steer me away from the action. "Come on, let's go outside," he said.

[Photo courtesy of Jay Leno]

Jay Leno with his parents, Angelo and Cathy.

My parents always made me feel secure. I can probably count the times on my hand that I came home to an empty house. If at three o'clock when I got home from school my mother wasn't home, my dad invariably was.

I remember in college, I brought home my grades from the semester and I showed them to my dad. He looked them over and was very impressed. He said, "Hey, this is a good report card. Now where do I sign it?" I said, "Dad, you don't sign it. I'm in college." He wouldn't have any of this. He said, "How is the teacher going to know I saw it?" I said, "The teacher doesn't care." He said, "What teacher doesn't care if I don't see the report card?" Not only did Dad sign the report card, he also made me bring it back to school to show my professors!

My dad always made me feel as if I was real special. I don't remember my father having a hobby. Growing up, all my dad did was do things for the family and with the family. He cut the lawn, he painted the house, and he spent time just being around us. It wasn't until I moved to California that I realized that all throughout his life *we* were his hobby.

◆ Jay Leno is the host of *The Tonight Show* on NBC.

Mark O'Meara

PGA Golfer

MY FATHER HAS ALWAYS BEEN IN THE
furniture business and his work
required that we move a lot. By
the time I was 13, I had lived in
North Carolina, Ohio, Michigan,
New York, Texas, and Illinois.
Dad finally settled our family in
Mission Viejo, California, and
that's when I took up golf at the
Mission Viejo Country Club.

My dad worked pretty darn
hard to provide a very nice way of
life for us. This often meant that he
had to travel somewhere all week
long for a furniture show. But
when he came home on the
weekend, he was devoted to us.
He'd hit golf balls with us or toss
around a football or even watch a
movie. Growing up, I always knew
that Dad's absences from home had
a purpose—making sure his family
had a comfortable life.

(Photo courtesy of International Management Group)

Mark O'Meara with his dad, Bob.

My dad is a pretty special
human being and I learned much from him by his example. He's lived his
life by the "Golden Rule"—he treats others in the same way he wants to be
treated. Dad is amazing at this. He's got a great personality and gets along
with everyone.

About 11 years ago, I traveled with my father to High Point, North
Carolina, to see firsthand how he goes about his business. In the two days I
spent at this furniture market, I saw many things. I never knew how hard

he worked. He went to work before dawn and left each day around nine o'clock in the evening. He never saw the sun! I also saw how much people loved my dad. Everywhere we went, it seemed that everyone not only knew my father, they respected him. My father is one of the most genuine people I know.

I played a lot of different sports growing up—hockey, baseball, tennis, and finally golf. The great thing about my father is that he didn't push me to pursue any one sport. He was most concerned about my happiness. I could have walked away from golf and he wouldn't have said a word. I think he would have been disappointed, but he would never have said, "Hey, you shouldn't do that." Dad taught me to take pride in what I do and like him, I'm very self-driven. As a result, he never had to tell me to practice or to go out and work on my game.

I also learned patience from my father, who has always been an extremely even-keeled person. I have been playing golf for 19 years, and it is just as frustrating now as when I first started playing. But my father taught me to put the game in its proper perspective. Every time I step on a golf course, I, of course, want to play well. On the other hand, I've learned that golf is not a life-or-death situation—even though sometimes we all make it that way! Dad taught me not to judge myself so harshly. As I've gotten older, I've come to appreciate what's most important in life—my wonderful wife and two great kids.

Dad has always been very proud of my accomplishments. And it's great when I get to share those moments with him. One of my greatest moments on the PGA Tour was when my father and I played together at the AT&T Pebble Beach National Pro-Am—and we won! It was such a thrill playing four days with my dad. I feel so fortunate to have had that experience. There aren't many other sports where a father and son can play together.

When I won the Masters, he was elated. And I think he gets a kick when people in his business congratulate him when I do well. My dad did so much to support me growing up and I am so glad that I have been able to turn around and return the favor. I couldn't have had a better dad.

◆ Mark O'Meara was a member of the victorious 1999 U.S. Ryder Cup team. In 1998, he won both the Masters Tournament and the British Open Championship. As a reward, he was chosen by his peers as Jack Nicklaus PGA Tour Player of the Year.

Martin Luther King III

President, SCLC

DADDY PREACHED IN CHURCH MANY of the same lessons that we learned at home. First and foremost, we were taught the "Golden Rule"—that one should treat your fellow human being as you would want to be treated.

In addition to that, we were taught to honor our parents and to love our neighbors. The greatest commodity in our home was love. Daddy used to bring home people all the time. He'd meet people in town, he'd call Mother in the afternoon and say, "I want to have three people join us for dinner." Mother never knew whether she was cooking for just the six of us or whether she might be cooking for fifteen! So the spirit of love was the most prevalent thing in our house. He was just incredibly giving.

(Family portrait courtesy of The Piece/Blount Agency)

Martin Luther King III with his family.

As a child, we had a normal routine. We knew that Daddy was traveling and trying to make our world better for all of God's children. So we became accustomed to the fact that he wasn't going to be home every night. When Daddy was home, we were so happy to see him. We didn't spend a large quantity of time together. But the quality of our time together was always excellent.

He taught us how to swim. We also used to ride bikes together from time to time. I still remember the last vacation we took together in 1967. Because he had to travel out of town soon, he took my brother Dexter and me to a hotel that was very close to the Atlanta airport. This hotel had a swimming pool and it was very exciting. I realize that by today's standards that wouldn't be a great vacation. But back then, whenever Daddy spent time with us, it meant so much and it was a big deal.

Honesty and integrity were certainly very core values that were instilled within our family. I remember when I was about five, we went to the airport to drop Daddy off to catch an airplane. I went into one of the souvenir shops and I wanted some crayons. They were on the shelf and were very appealing to me as a child. So I just picked them up. Subconsciously I must have known that it was wrong because I was so embarrassed. Daddy soon saw what I had in my possession and he made me go back, return the crayons and apologize. And so at a very early age, although I did things kids do, I learned the difference between right and wrong and how one should behave.

I think every child goes through a particular period of struggle and I think the most important thing that a parent can provide is a foundation. In my family it was a moral and spiritual foundation. In life, one goes through all types of adversity. Daddy taught us that we're going to succeed some days and we're going to fail some days and that's how life is. The measure of succeeding in life is to be able to overcome adversity. If we did not have the spiritual foundation that was instilled by my mother and daddy, I think that we, as children, would have failed on many occasions.

I believe that foundation is what helped Daddy to endure through times of difficulty. When my daddy came out against the Vietnam War, the whole civil rights community went against him and could not understand why he would take on an international crisis that—in their minds—had nothing to do with civil or human rights. In fact, it had everything to do with human rights. These leaders would say, "President Johnson has been good to us. He's signed the Civil Rights Act. He's signed the Voting Rights Act. Why would you be critical of him?" He was, in a sense, isolated. But he stood up with his own convictions. He said, "This is wrong and I must stand up against it—because injustice anywhere is a threat to justice everywhere." As a result, it was a lonely road. So Daddy had to turn to prayer. He had to turn to his basic foundation of faith.

I think he would be pleased to know that I was heading the Southern Christian Leadership Council—an organization that he co-founded in 1957. But he would probably be very disappointed that many of the issues that he addressed over 31 years ago are still within our midst. And many of those issues have, in fact, grown in intensity. For example, violence is at epidemic levels. Poverty continues—even though this is the greatest period of prosperity in this country. I also think that he'd be saddened by the fact that instead of moving forward it seems that we're regressing in certain areas. It does not mean that we've not come a long way, it just means that unfortunately, we still have a long, long way to go.

I look at my father in two regards. First and foremost, he was Daddy. He was—in my judgment—an outstanding father to us. But now as an adult, I also see him as the incredible human rights leader that he was. It's a tremendous honor and blessing to be a part of a legacy that's so phenomenal. Daddy was unpretentious and he was tremendously humble. He was very focused and he felt spiritually directed. But he still maintained the ability to communicate with people at all levels—whether they were in the streets or whether they were in suites. He could go into a pool hall and shoot a game of pool with the hustlers and be just as comfortable going into a corporate suite and communicating with a CEO. Today, if we could embrace the philosophy that he advocated of nonviolence and treating others with respect, our nation and world would be an extraordinary place.

◆ Martin Luther King III is the second oldest of the four children of Dr. Martin Luther King, Jr. and Coretta Scott King. He is the president of the Southern Christian Leadership Conference, the organization that his father co-founded in 1957.

John McCain

U.S. Senator, Arizona (R)

I GREW UP IN A MILITARY FAMILY. MY FATHER AND MY GRANDFATHER WERE BOTH Navy admirals and I continued the tradition of service to my country. I went to the Naval Academy and became a naval aviator. The biggest impact my father had on me was that he had very high standards of honorable behavior. And he always strove to impart those standards to me.

My father, for example, believed that the most serious offense a person could commit was to betray or not live up to the qualities of leadership that the people who served under him had a right to expect. That meant honesty, integrity, and never, ever doing anything that would set a bad example for them. My father was known as a sailor's kind of officer. He was very much loved by the enlisted people who served under him. Although he was a tough disciplinarian, he was at the same time very concerned about their well-being and their morale. He knew every sailor on every ship that he ever commanded. He spent an enormous amount of time with the people he called blue-jackets, which is a very antiquated term for sailors.

Duty, honor, country—these were the values that were the foundation of his entire life. His one guiding principle, though, was the Golden Rule—do unto others as you would have them do unto you. He said, "It takes moral courage to issue an unpopular order and then to make sure of its execution." That was his first and last principle of leadership.

When he was a three-star admiral, he was not complacent. He was obviously ambitious and aspired to be a four-star admiral. At this point in his career the Pentagon sent him to a job in New York at the United Nations, which was universally regarded as a dead end to a military career. Nobody who had ever gone to that job had been promoted to the four-star rank. I remember talking to him about it, and he was neither pessimistic or in any way depressed. He said, "Son, no matter what the job is, if you do the very best you can, then you are going to succeed."

And indeed, after he had been at the United Nations for a few years, he was promoted to four-star admiral and was sent to command U.S. Naval forces in Europe. After that, he was promoted to be commander in chief of all

U.S. forces in the Pacific during the Vietnam War.

My father told me never to dishonor my country any more than I would dishonor my name. In 1967, I was shot down during a bombing mission over Hanoi and taken prisoner by the Vietnamese.

They offered to release me early in 1968. This was clearly a propaganda move on their part because my father was commander in chief of U.S. forces in the Pacific. I nearly accepted the communists' offer. But there were a number of considerations that convinced me to reject the offer and remain in prison until the war's end. The main consideration was the effect it would have on my fellow prisoners and on my father's regard for me.

(Photo courtesy of John McCain)

John McCain with his dad, Admiral Sidney McCain, Jr.

Our code of conduct in Vietnam said that people should be released according to their order of capture. I had arrived some two and a half years after Everett Alvarez, Jr., who was the first P.O.W. I was beaten for refusing to return home. My lowest moment came when, at the end of my rope, I signed a false confession to crimes against North Vietnam. I was ashamed. I felt I had embarrassed not only my country but also my father and my grandfather.

My father heard about my confession from naval intelligence sources. In my first meeting with him after five and a half years of captivity, we embraced. "I'm proud of you," he said. "You did the best you could, John. That's all that's expected of any of us."

My father taught me more than to always do the right thing. My father taught me to know what the right thing is.

◆ After a 22-year career in the U.S. Navy and two terms as U.S. representative (1982–86), John McCain was elected to the U.S. Senate in 1986 and re-elected in 1992 and 1998. He is chairman of the Senate Commerce, Science, and Transportation Committee.

Gene Cernan

Astronaut

I GREW UP ABOUT 18 MILES WEST OF CHICAGO. THERE WAS NO EISENHOWER Freeway back then. We lived out in what they called "the sticks."

My father unfortunately never had a chance to get a college education. As a matter of fact, he literally finished high school through a correspondence course. But he was one of those guys who was self-educated and could literally do anything. He could fix your stuffed toilet, he could build your garage, he could rewire your house, and he could tear your automobile engine apart. And we did all those things together when I was a kid growing up. He never said this to me, but I think he would have wanted the education that would have allowed him to be an engineer. That's of course, where he focused and directed me. My dad was determined that my sister and I both get the education that he never had.

Dad never forced me to do anything. He just asked me to do my best. He said, "All I'm ever going to ask of you, son, is to do your best. Whether it's on the football field, in the classroom, or in whatever you choose to do in life—just do your best." But he added a caveat. He said, "There's only one person who knows what their best really is and that's you." I've never forgotten that.

When I was about 10 years old, I helped my father build a new garage. I pounded some nails into a two-by-four and as I was hammering away, I bent a few nails. My dad wasn't looking, so I tried to get away with it by pounding them into the board anyway. Well, my dad took a look at my work at the end of the afternoon and saw what I had done. Rather than get angry, he made me pull out each of those nails. He then told me to straighten them out and put those same damn nails back in the same damn holes! This was not very easy. But Dad taught me this life lesson as a little boy: "If you're going to do anything, do it right the first time."

From an early age, my sights were set on flying airplanes off of aircraft carriers. The combination of my dad wanting me to go to a good school and me wanting me to fly in the Navy led me to an N.R.O.T.C. scholarship at Purdue.

Because my father worked at a torpedo facility, he would see young officers running around in uniforms all the time. So when I got commissioned at Purdue, that was a big-time day for him. All of a sudden his son was wearing the stripes of an ensign. His chest was sticking out. He was very excited, happy, and proud.

The next big achievement for me was when I got my wings. He understood my ambition and was really in tune with what I was doing and why I was doing it. When he visited me in Pensacola, I got to take him aboard an aircraft carrier. It was a thrill for me that I could begin to share some of my life with him. If you ever felt that you wanted to repay your parents for all they've done for you, it's by making them proud.

When I finally flew in space on Gemini 9, he just bubbled. I felt like maybe for the first time in my entire life, I could say thank you to my dad for the things that I didn't even know I was learning from him at the time I was growing up. He didn't live to see me go to the moon on Apollo X nor was he around for Apollo XVII. He died way too early.

Gene Cernan with his dad, Andrew.

It was a sense of regret that he never got to see me achieve those things. But it made me more determined to go back on Apollo XVII and not just walk on the moon, but get command of my own flight. I was driven to do that. But in some way or another, I think he knows I went.

My father just loved the outdoors and I've got a little ranch in the hill country of Texas, west of San Antonio. I sit out on the porch often and just look out and see how beautiful it is. There are horses, deer, and longhorns out there and the breezes that come up on the porch are just wonderful. But I would give a lifetime to have my dad sit out there with me for one weekend. I would almost kill for that kind of opportunity.

The thing I regret most is that I never realized how important my father was to me in my life in steering me in the right direction—and how much I truly loved him—until he was gone. I keep thinking, "Golly, if I could only have him back for a little while." I'd love to share with him the things I have because of what he did for me. If you could recreate a little bit of time and package it, and save it for a time like now, it would be special. He gave me the values that I have. I am who I am and achieved what I did because of my father. He's the real hero.

◆ Captain Eugene A. Cernan is chairman of Johnson Engineering Corporation, which provides NASA Johnson Space Center with engineering, design, and development services in support of the Space Shuttle, the Space Station, and future space flight projects. As Commander of Apollo XVII, he holds the distinction of being the last man to leave his footprints on the surface of the moon.

Maureen Reagan

Political Analyst

WHEN DAD LOST THE REPUBLICAN NOMINATION IN KANSAS CITY IN 1976, I was just devastated. I cried for two days. I just couldn't stop. And every time he saw me during that period he'd say, "Are you still crying?" He was trying his best to cheer me up, but to no avail. As the convention was closing, he pulled me into this meeting room and he told me, "There's a reason for this. I don't know what it is. But there's a reason." And he always believed that. Dad was the eternal optimist. He has always quoted his mother, Nell: "When one door closes, another one opens." Everything happens for a reason.

My father is an incredible competitor. It just doesn't always show. When we got off the plane in Los Angeles after the convention, I had one picture left in my camera and as Dad and Nancy started to get in the car, I said, "Let's finish this roll. I have one more picture." He whispered to me, "Hurry up, my face is starting to hurt." And I knew then that he was using every ounce of energy he had to hold it together for the rest of us. He has always had great faith and has always believed that God has a plan. He'd say, "If you just keep doing what you're doing, the path is going to open up and you'll see what it is you're supposed to do."

My father also had a way of dealing with things with great humor. He never underestimated me and he never spoke down to me—even as a child. When I was about four and a half, it was time to go to first grade and I announced to my dad that I was not going to go to school. My dad, of course, wanted to know why. I explained, "I know what I want to be when I grow up. I want to be a great actress. And you go to school to learn what you want to be. Since I already know what I want to be, I don't need to go to school." Dad listened to me and thought about that for a minute.

Rather than express disappointment or anger, Dad simply said, "Well I'm thrilled to know that you will never be bedeviled by uncertainty. However, you're going to need to learn to read and write if you're going to be a great actress. You'll have to read scripts. You'll have to read contracts." And I replied, "You can read them to me."

Dad smiled. "Well I can't think of anything that I'd rather do in life than follow you around, reading to you all the things that you need. But what if I'm suddenly not there one day and you had to suddenly have a change in your script or you had a meeting and I wasn't around? You'd be so embarrassed."

Well I thought about that. And while I was thinking, he said, "And you have to learn how to write. Think about it—you have to learn how to sign those contracts. And, of course, you'll need to know how to sign autographs."

So the very first day in school I told the teacher I wanted to learn how to sign my name. Years later as I was coming out the back stage of a theatre a woman came up to me and asked if I would mind signing my autograph. And I said, "Mind? It's the only reason I went to school!"

Dad spoke to me in a language I could understand and that's a great talent. Whether he was talking to kings or prime ministers, waiters or taxi drivers, he always talked to people the same and treated them the same. I can see why he got the best of the Soviets. He's a great human being and I miss him terribly.

◆ Maureen Reagan, the eldest daughter of former President Ronald Reagan, is a political analyst, talk show host, best-selling author, and a member of the Alzheimer's Association's National Board of Directors.

(Photo courtesy of Maureen Reagan)

Maureen Reagan with her dad, Ronald.

Anthony Fauci, M.D.

Director, National Institute of Allergy and Infectious Diseases

MY FATHER IS A FIRST GENERATION Italian-American who had a very strong sense of public service and a strong sense of integrity. When I was eight years old, he bought, with the help of his father, his own pharmacy. It was a classic situation—we lived on top of the drugstore. I was always impressed by the fact that he worked so hard. His hours were extraordinary. He would open the store around nine o'clock in the morning and he would then be in the store until ten o'clock at night—six days a week (and half a day on Sundays). Despite these long hours, we were a very close-knit, happy family. As was the case with many Italian families, every Sunday afternoon we had a big family dinner—either at our house or at the house of one of our grandparents who lived nearby.

(Photo courtesy of Dr. Anthony Fauci)

Dr. Anthony Fauci with his dad, Steven Anthony.

My father is a very moral, ethical, and religious man. I remember that when I was a child he tried to organize the pharmacists in the neighborhood into the Catholic Pharmacists Guild, for the purpose of promoting high standards of integrity and ethics among the pharmacies. It wasn't anything related to money-making. Rather, it was more about good practices and attending to the needs of the customers.

Dad was generous to a fault when it came to accommodating patients who couldn't afford to pay their bill. He kept a running account for those who couldn't pay—much to the chagrin of the whole family. My sister and I would say, "Dad, come on!" And Dad never listened. He'd say, "They can't afford it. We'll just put it on the bill." Weeks and months would go by before these bills were paid off. Still, Dad made just enough at the pharmacy to get by in a way that we had the comforts of being able to eat enough and dress reasonably well.

Dad's store eventually became a combination doctor's office, pharmacy, and psychiatrist's couch. He was constantly taking care of the people in the neighborhood. They would come to talk to him about everything from how to take their medications, to being consoled over the death of a loved one, to marital problems.

Everything in my formative years was geared toward the concept of public service. My father taught me early on in life that because I had the gifts of high intelligence, high energy, and good health, that it's my responsibility to do something for people. There was almost no emphasis placed on making money. That was something that was a nonentity in the family discussions. In fact, it was never a consideration in anybody's decision about anything. And it had a very important impact on me. I learned from him that it is important to devote one's life to something with impact—something that could be used for the greater good. My decisions in life to enter the field of medicine, to go into public service, even the fact that I have never charged a patient for anything since I became a physician in 1966 all stem from the lessons I learned at home. My father's theme all along was very much oriented to taking care of other people as opposed to taking care of yourself.

My father strove to do good things for people and to be a good person. He was a role model of goodness.

◆ Dr. Anthony Fauci is director of the National Institute of Allergy and Infectious Diseases. He is one of the world's leaders in AIDS research.

Gail Devers

Olympic Track Champion

TELEVISION WAS NOT ENCOURAGED WHEN I WAS GROWING UP. MY FATHER WAS a minister at the Mount Erie Baptist Church in San Diego and one of the few TV shows I was permitted to watch was *I Love Lucy*. And did I ever love Lucy! I thought she was hilarious. In fact, I wanted to invite her to my house for a sleep-over party.

When I was six, I started pleading with my father to arrange a meeting with my idol. He tried reasoning with me. "Lucy is not a real person. That's a program and Lucy's just a character," he said. "Do not believe everything you see on television." Of course I did not listen and continued my whining. Dad finally gave in and agreed to drive me the 120 miles to meet "Lucy." Little did I know what he really had in mind.

After driving all over Hollywood we finally passed an older lady whom Dad pointed to and said, "That's Lucy!"

I burst into tears. "That's not Lucy. She doesn't look like that on TV." Dad pulled the car over, calmed me down, and gently explained, "Lucy is a fantasy, an illusion." He then paused, looked me straight in the eye, and said, "I want you to be real."

This is one of the most valuable pieces of advice I have ever received. Over the years, Dad's words became increasingly important to me. Being "real" meant knowing who I was, being true to myself, and standing up for my beliefs. I realized that if I wanted other people to respect me, I had to respect myself first.

My father also helped me develop self-confidence by letting me set my own goals. For example, he never pressured me to run track and field. It was my decision and he encouraged me. At track meets other parents boasted that their children were going to be lawyers or doctors. Dad simply said, "Gail will give her best effort to whatever she decides to do."

Through his patient and thoughtful words Dad was handing me the keys to living an honest, principled life. His advice and, more importantly, example enabled me to strive for excellence. My father helped me discover my full potential and for that I am forever grateful. Thanks Dad, and "Lucy," for your lessons that have lasted a lifetime.

◆ Gail Devers is a world-class sprinter and hurdler who won gold medals in the 100-meter dash and the 400-meter relay at the 1996 Summer Olympic Games in Atlanta. She won the 100-meter hurdles at the 1999 World Championships for the third time and continues training for the 2000 Summer Olympics in Sydney, Australia.

(Photo courtesy of Elite International Sports Marketing)

Gail Devers jumping hurdles.

Barry Levinson

Film Director

MY FATHER WAS IN THE DISCOUNT APPLIANCE BUSINESS IN BALTIMORE, AND I used to go down to his store quite a bit. In fact, when I was a teenager, I used to actually work in his store. I should use the word "work" lightly because I couldn't sell a refrigerator if my life depended on it! My father, however, was an extraordinary salesman. He was able to walk over to a complete stranger and somehow pleasantly engage them in conversation. Fast talking and hustling were not his style. He sold in a very simple and quiet fashion. In a business that had its fair share of duplicitous salesmen, my father stood out. He was very straightforward and incredibly honest.

When I was growing up, I looked to my father for guidance. But I also admired him in a very superficial sense. He was always a wonderful dresser! His pants would break just above the shoe, his ties were knotted perfectly and his shirts were always pressed just right. I got a kick out of watching him get ready for work!

The greatest thing my father gave me was his unconditional support. I was 23 when I decided to move out to California to pursue a career in show business. I had been working in a nice job in local television and was starting to make a decent living. I was definitely taking a chance and many people questioned whether I was making a practical decision. But my father never questioned me.

He simply said, "It's your choice and I'm sure that you'll do all right." He had an incredible amount of faith in the choices that I made and had enough belief in me to allow me to do what I had to do.

My father didn't profess to understand this business on any level. When I first arrived in Los Angeles, I spent several months just writing material. I had written quite a bit, but had yet to sell anything.

As a true businessman, my father said to me, "Well, at least you've got inventory." In his mind, having excess supply was a good thing! But he also gave me a little extra money when times were tough.

Conversely, at a certain point, when I had sold everything that I had written, my father said, "Well, it looks like you're out of inventory!"

As my career began to take off, my dad was very proud of my achievements. He wouldn't always tell me directly, though. Often I would hear about it through friends.

But on one of my trips back to Baltimore, I brought home the Emmy that I won for "The Carol Burnett Show." When I gave it to my parents, I could see that my father was very excited.

What was good about our relationship is that we didn't have to agree on everything. What was important was that we understood and respected each other. He trusted me and always allowed me to pursue my interests. I think that was very beneficial.

Another thing that was great growing up is that I was raised not only by my mom and dad, but also by a large extended family. I grew up with my mother, my father, my sister, and my grandmother and grandfather all under the same roof. I even had cousins, aunts, and uncles up the street. This extended family provided me with a huge support system. I think children look to their fathers for support.

I never wanted overt guidance from my father; I just wanted to know that he was there. My father had a quiet strength, and he provided that support for me time and time again.

◆ Barry Levinson is an Academy Award–winning film director. *Wag the Dog, Rain Man, Sleepers, Diner,* and *Avalon* are among his critically acclaimed films.

(Photo courtesy of Sphere)

Barry Levinson with his dad, Irvin.

Jesse Jackson, Jr.

U. S. Representative, Illinois (D)

THERE WAS A DYNAMIC THAT EXISTED IN OUR HOUSEHOLD THAT FOSTERED learning, growth, and development. From an early age my dad taught us that we all had purpose and that our purpose was part of a much larger plan. He would often say, "To whom much is given, much is required." It's a biblical concept that gave us the sense that we had been extremely blessed.

Every Christmas was spent with inmates at the Cook County Jail in Chicago. We would go to the jail with a choir and we would do an annual Christmas service for the prisoners. As a young boy, I really wanted to be sitting at home under my Christmas tree playing with my toys. But over the years, I came to understand and appreciate this noble cause. The lesson I learned was that we were extremely blessed to have two parents who loved us so much. We were also very fortunate to have a father who was not involved in the criminal justice system because of anything he had done.

When I was growing up most of my friends in elementary school knew who we were before we knew who they were. As a result, there was always this challenge to get to know people who were sincere in their desire to befriend us. I've inherited my father's friends and I've also inherited my father's detractors. But my father has always said to me, "You've earned neither. You have to work real hard to prove your friendship and you have to work even harder to show detractors that you have something to say."

My dad put leg weights in all of my shoes in order to keep me grounded. Growing up in Chicago, the home to the left of us was owned by a very famous African-American entertainer who had seven children. They bought two new Cadillacs every year, the kids had go-carts, and they received everything you can imagine for Christmas. None of the seven children ended up graduating from college and two of them are in and out of jail.

The home to our right was a family with two boys. One night at three o'clock in the morning my father woke my brother and me up from a dead sleep. He took us to his bathroom window and had us stand on the toilet and look out the window.

"What do you see over there?" he asked.

It was Peter Fozert and his brother. They were each reading, hunched over lights at their desks. Today both of them are medical doctors and Ph.D.s. Even as a small boy, the message of that night was clear to me. We needed to study hard and develop our own minds.

My father instilled in me the idea that no matter what we wanted to be, we had a calling that was higher than our own personal ambition. If I wanted to be a doctor, that wouldn't be enough. I should aim at being Surgeon General, where I could be concerned with health care for everybody. The idea was to get in a position where we could help the most people.

My interest in the environment, justice, labor rights, and fighting for an increase in the minimum wage didn't come out of nowhere. I didn't just wake up one day and say those were great issues. I saw my father

(Photo Credit: Daily Southtown/Chicago)

Jesse Jackson, Jr. with his dad, Jesse Jackson, Sr.

fighting for more participation on the Chicago School Board. I saw him fighting for inner-city schools to get the same type of resources that suburban schools were getting. I saw Reverend Jackson take on hospitals that wouldn't admit minorities who didn't have health insurance in emergency situations. I simply applied what I grew up with and saw to my own work in Congress.

I have an older sister, two brothers, and a younger sister, and my parents fostered a sense of home and a sense of character development in each one of us. I speak to my dad several times a day and I refer to him as Reverend. When I'm broke, though, or I'm short on money, he becomes Dad real quick!

◆ Congressman Jesse Jackson, Jr. represents the 2nd District of Illinois in the U.S. House of Representatives.

John McEnroe

Captain, U.S. Davis Cup Team

MY PARENTS HAVE BEEN TOGETHER 41 YEARS AND IN ALL THAT TIME THERE was never a moment when I thought their marriage wasn't going to work out. It just always felt like they were a team. Of course there was a lot of yelling around the house. But we're Irish-Catholic New Yorkers, so this was all completely normal!

What kids want most, I think, is to know that they have their mother and father behind them—supporting them—on a regular basis. We had this growing up. There was a certain level of comfort in knowing that they were always there for me and my brothers.

When I was about 15 years old, I attended a very famous tennis academy in New York. One semester, I took part in some high school antics along with a number of other students. No one got hurt and it was nothing that would put you in jail, but it was stuff that was inappropriate and stupid, and big enough to warrant a six-month suspension from this tennis academy!

I learned of my suspension from my parents and I was devastated. I thought to myself, they're really gonna give it to me. But their reaction was the exact opposite. Even though they were pissed off at me, they completely supported me. As a matter of fact they were mad at the guy who ran the academy. I think it was because they realized that despite my mistake, I was a decent kid. I felt a level of support that day that I'll never forget. We never went back to that tennis academy and we never looked back. We simply moved forward with another coach.

When I left Stanford after my freshman year, once again I had something that a 19-year-old kid needs—the full support of my parents. My dad realized that turning pro was a once-in-a-lifetime opportunity. He saw how much I had matured in my first year at school, and at the end of the academic year my dad said to me, "It's time to do this." Those words meant a lot to me.

There was never any doubt that my father loved me. He lived through his kids. He didn't do things for himself on the weekend. Instead, he would take us to play tennis, CYO basketball, or baseball. We sensed the joy he got from that.

From an early age, we knew and appreciated how hard Dad worked. Initially, he worked two jobs in order to provide for us. I still get chills when I think back to the day he made partner in his law firm. I was probably 14 at the time and it was like winning Wimbledon for him! I know how many years he worked towards that goal and how much it meant to him. I was just so happy for my dad.

I've always hated losing. That goes without saying! But my father taught me that you always get another chance around the corner. My most enjoyable years on the circuit were the early years where I felt I learned from my mistakes. That attitude goes back to the way I was brought up. When I would lose a match as a kid, my father was always there to console me. He'd say, "I know you can do it, son." Sometimes I just didn't want to hear that. But I came to realize that he believed in me more than I believed in myself. In a subtle, healthy way, he pushed me to succeed and to reach my maximum potential. He somehow managed to do this without applying any pressure. Without a doubt, I know that my dad is the reason that I am where I am today.

◆ John McEnroe is a member of the International Tennis Hall of Fame, the captain of the U.S Davis Cup team, and a commentator for NBC Sports, CBS Sports, and the USA network.

(Photo courtesy of John and Kay McEnroe)

John McEnroe and family.

Victoria Gotti

Novelist

THERE'S A LOT ABOUT MY FATHER THAT THE PUBLIC DOESN'T KNOW. HE AND his 12 brothers and sisters grew up under very difficult conditions and experienced a very tough life. But he always tried to shield us from that. He strived to make our lives better. Closeness and bonding with each other were most important to him.

Even though we weren't a wealthy family growing up, my father was always doing for the next person. He couldn't turn down anyone who would ask him a favor and he would always offer to lend a hand. I remember there was a boy in the neighborhood who had cancer and had to have the bottom part of his leg amputated. The boy's parents didn't have money for the prosthetic, but my father went out and made sure he had one. They loved him for that. He never looked for adulation or anything in return. That's just part of his generous nature.

When the Good Humor Ice Cream truck would come to the neighborhood, it would always ring the bell in front of our house. That was the signal for all the kids in the neighborhood to drop what they were doing and come over to our driveway. Dad would buy them all ice cream. It was like a big party and the kids just loved him. We got a big kick out of it too!

My father always let us know when he was proud of our accomplishments. When I graduated from the sixth grade, at the closing exercises there was a special award that went out to the most studious person in the class. It was the annual United Federation of Teachers Award, and it was always a big deal. I had won quite a few awards that morning, but this was the last one given out. When the principal announced my name, I saw my father's face. He was the proudest person in the world. I can still see today how big his smile was.

After driving home, my mom and my brothers and sister got out of the car and I gathered up all of my awards to take inside.

"Oh, leave those here," my father said.

Dad took those awards around the entire neighborhood for the entire day—to every store he shopped at and to every person he knew. He just showed off my accomplishments to everybody. I thought it was the funniest thing. All these years later, I still hear about that day from friends in our neighborhood. And my father still laughs whenever I bring it up to him.

(Photo Credit: Anthony Loew. Courtesy of Crown Publishing Company)

Victoria Gotti

The most important thing I received from my father was strength. It wasn't that I wasn't allowed to cry growing up, but Dad taught me what was worth getting upset about. He taught me the difference between a monumental disappointment and a minute one. When I came to him with a skinned knee or a crisis at school, he'd say, "Listen, have yourself a good cry. But this is not tragic. Save your tears for some day—God forbid—when you really need them. And I hope you'll never need them." Unfortunately, in my life, I've needed them. But I understand now why he said what he said. And boy, did he know what he was talking about!

My father always dealt with disappointment in his life amazingly well. He taught me that you just have to move on and not dwell on things that don't work out.

"There are things in life that you just can't change," he'd say. "There are choices in life and you have to make those choices. Good or bad, every choice has consequences."

I don't think I could have learned those lessons from anybody else.

We also learned to never feel pity for ourselves. Time and time again, he'd tell us that there are so many people in this world who are much worse off. Dad taught us that we are gifted to have such a loving family.

In the Italian culture, tradition rules all. Sunday dinner was always very big in our family. There were no excuses for an absence. You had to be there. That was a big thing with my father. What meant the most to him was that we all stay close. Even now, he'll still say to me in letters, on the telephone, or on a visit, "When was the last time the family was together?"

He loves the fact that we've all lived close to one another through the years. And now the Sunday dinners revolve around my house. It's scary because they say there comes a time in your life when you look in the mirror and you've become your mother. Well, I feel like I've become my father! Like my father, family is the most important thing to me.

When I see a headline about my father, I'll usually skip the story. It's not the man I know. The man I know is wise, strong, and compassionate. He always encouraged me and made me want to achieve and excel.

I try to see my father once every month. But it's not easy. We have to fly to St. Louis and then drive two and a half hours. And then you're in the middle of nowhere. It's also very difficult knowing that my father is in prison. But I think there's a lot in life that I have to be thankful for and a lot that I have to be thankful for because of him.

◆ Victoria Gotti is a best-selling novelist whose forthcoming book, *Superstar*, will be published in August 2000. She is the daughter of reputed Mafia kingpin, John Gotti.

Drew Bledsoe

Quarterback, New England Patriots

I GREW UP IN A FAMILY FULL OF OPTIMISTS. MY FATHER, IN PARTICULAR, instilled this "glass is half full" attitude in me. He always liked to say, "Happiness is an attitude of choice." Dad meant that regardless of what is going on in your life, when you wake up in the morning you should choose to be happy. That's how my parents live their lives. Obviously, there are times when you are going to go through tough circumstances, and you can't be cheerful all day, every day. But for the most part, my parents, regardless of what was happening, raised my brother and me in a wonderful atmosphere. My parents are married and still love each other. So, compared to 90 percent of the world, it seems, we had an ideal household.

Their outlook on life has helped me confront a lot of things in life, but especially how to deal with the stressful world of professional football. As a quarterback I have to be an optimist and live my life almost in denial. If I ever took a realistic look at some of the situations I'm faced with as an athlete, I would have to give up. The odds can sometimes be insurmountable. But as a quarterback, rather than looking at what kind of desperate situation I'm in, I try to look at how I will come through and win the game. I think that is the way you have to be if you are going to be successful in anything you do.

The biggest thing that my parents did was tell me from a very early age that I didn't have to earn their love. They were going to love me no matter what. That really allowed me a lot of freedom in my personal life and in the rest of my life as well. In high school, I wanted to try to win every football game. But it wasn't because I felt like I had to do that to try to please my parents. They were going to stand by me whether we won or lost or whether or not I *even* played football.

I learned much from my father by just watching his example. He taught me that if you tell the truth and are straightforward with people, most of the time they'll be honest with you. I also learned not to let people walk all over you and to stand up for what you believe in, regardless of the situation.

"You'll be satisfied with yourself, as long as you stand by the things that you believe in," Dad said.

In high school, my relationship with my father grew even stronger. He was one of my football coaches and one of the best people you could ever find to teach the game of football. He managed to get the best out of people time and time again through praise. He was extremely patient and rarely got frustrated, which is very hard to do when you are dealing with 50 players who have different skill levels. My father was "coach" at school, but once we got home, he became "Dad" again. Over dinner, we'd talk about the team and he always respected my opinion.

Since I've been playing quarterback, I've learned from my dad that much is expected from my position. He taught me that as a leader I can't ask somebody to do something that I'm not willing to do myself. Like my father, I've always chosen to lead by example. My father also taught me never to criticize somebody else's performance until I have looked at my own first. These lessons were about how to play the game. But my dad

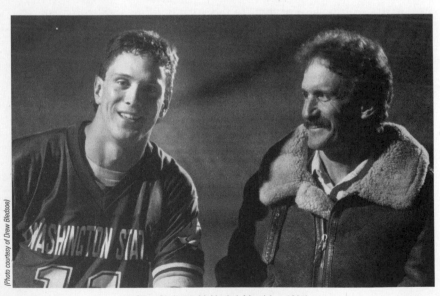

(Photo courtesy of Drew Bledsoe)

Drew Bledsoe with his dad, Mac (circa 1991).

never put any pressure on me on how I played the game. He just said, "Do your best. All that matters at the end of the day is whether you met your own standards."

Losing the Super Bowl was a great disappointment. But I learned from my dad to put things in their proper perspective. It's only natural to have setbacks in life. But you deal with them and you move on. If losing the Super Bowl is the greatest disappointment I have in my life, then I will have lived a very blessed life.

Many kids look to sports figures as their heroes, but when I was in third grade I wrote my dad a letter that said all I ever wanted to do in my whole life was to be just like him. I admired everything about him. As far as I knew he was perfect. My mom saved that letter. And although I now know that my dad's not perfect, one thing has remained constant—he's my biggest hero.

◆ Drew Bledsoe is the All-Pro quarterback for the New England Patriots.

Brian McKnight

Grammy-Nominated R&B Singer

MY DAD CAME FROM NOTHING, SO HE ALWAYS WANTED TO MAKE OUR LIVES better. When I was about 10 years old, we moved to Orlando from Buffalo so that my father could take a job with Lockheed Martin in their aerospace division.

Every day as I got up for school, Dad left for work. It may not seem like a great accomplishment, but there's not too many of my friends that can say that they had a father who did that. It was just amazing to me.

My parents divorced when I was 12 years old and my brothers and I lived with my mom. After the divorce, Dad did everything he could to let us know that he still loved us very much. Every time I did anything, he was there. He'd make it a point to come to most of my games and he was louder than anybody! Despite the divorce, he was always there when I needed him.

I think that the biggest thing my dad instilled in us was to have pride in our work. Dad always said, "If you aren't going to try to be the best, then don't try it at all."

This attitude applied to everything we did, but especially sports. When I was seven years old, I played little league pee-wee football. One game, Dad thought I was really slacking off in the first half. So after halftime, he came into the huddle and kicked me—literally—in my butt!

He said, "If you're not going to do the best that you can, then we're going home."

I listened to what my dad said and I did what I needed to do. I wanted to prove to him that I could be everything he thought I could be. It was like that in everything. The worst thing that we could have done growing up was disappoint our parents. So I just learned how to make them proud.

I was on the basketball team in ninth grade and in one of our first games, I played my heart out. I scored almost thirty points in a losing cause. When my father took me home from the gym, I was heartbroken.

I cried in the car all the way home. As we got in our driveway, Dad finally spoke up.

He said, "Brian, you played well. In fact, you played great. There's no reason for you to get so upset."

I learned a lot from that night in ninth grade. All that my father ever asked of me was to do the best that I can. I apply that lesson to what I do now. The focus that I have in my life is all because of how he treated us when we were small.

I have two children now and it's scary. My methods may be a little different from my father's, but I'm instilling in them the same values that I learned from my dad. I have become my father! I couldn't have had a better role model.

(Photo Credit: Faindee St. Nicholas. Courtesy of Motown Records.)

Brian McKnight

◆ Brian McKnight is a Grammy-nominated recording artist with the Motown label. He has been called "one of the finest pop singers alive" by the *New York Times*.

Steve Forbes

President and Editor-in-Chief, *Forbes Magazine*

MY FATHER HAD A WONDERFUL SENSE OF THE RHYTHMS OF LIFE. WHEN WE were growing up he was a firm disciplinarian who taught my brothers, my sister, and me what was right and what was wrong. But he also gave us a tremendous amount of independence and let us develop our own personalities. I remember two of my brothers back in those years decided to forget what bathtubs and showers were invented for. They let their hair grow to their knees! Despite their odd appearance, my father never said, "Don't do it." He obviously didn't like it, but his attitude was that we had to learn from our own experiences.

When I was nine years old, I badly wanted to get a shotgun and learn how to shoot skeet. My father was adamantly against the idea. He had been in World War II as a machine gunner and was badly wounded, so since then he wanted nothing to do with weapons. He also thought I was much too young to take up something like that. But I persisted. Persistence often paid off with my father. It showed him that you really wanted something badly. One Christmas I received a fantastic 20-gauge Baretta shotgun. He made sure that I learned to use it and use it safely. He emphasized to me what his father always emphasized to him: "With possessions come responsibilities." Dad made certain that I got the most out of my new shotgun.

He also had a very good sense of how to talk to us as we got older. In the early '60s, the Surgeon General came out with a report saying that cigarette smoking was lethal. My father at the time was smoking almost four packs of cigarettes a day. When the report came out, he stopped smoking cigarettes cold turkey and never took them up again. Like my peers at that age, I was experimenting with cigarettes. I assumed in those days—I was about 15 at the time—that cigarette smoking was simply a part of becoming a grown-up. My father knew otherwise. He said, "I am not going to tell you not to smoke. But I am going to *ask* you not to do it."

Unlike other parents, he promised no reward if I quit. He simply said "You shouldn't smoke for the sake of your health." The manner in which he made his request made me feel, as the cliché goes, like a man. And I never puffed a cigarette again.

My father was a very vibrant man who had an infectious and vibrant spirit. I think his generous approach to life had an enormous impact on all of us. He had his share of setbacks and he had his share of pain. But we learned from him that you deal with those things, you put them behind you, and you move on. You don't pine or whine or say what might have been. His attitude was, "There's always tomorrow."

Dad also showed us a lighter side that was very special. When we were young, during the summer, we would go out west to Wyoming. Mom and Dad took the station wagon, five kids, two dogs, and maybe one other person. During the four-day drive to Wyoming, Dad would get a mischievous look in his eye and he would see how fast the car would go to my mother's absolute horror—and to our utter delight. Sometimes he would play games like seeing if we could make it to the hotel without

Steve Forbes and his family (circa 1952).

gassing up. Because he was a firm individual, these little escapades were an absolute delight to us.

Many of the rules he espoused would be learned at church, which we went to every Sunday. I remember as a kid I would ask him, "Why do we have to go to church on Sunday?" I told him that it should be my decision. But he would have no part of that. He said, "I am making you go to church so at least you will have something to rebel against when you get older. I don't want you to have any illusions of what is right and what is wrong. I want you to know what the rules are and you can take it from there."

My father also wanted us at an early age to know where our bread is buttered. He would say, "If you think you've arrived in life, then you are ready to be shown the door. Nothing stays the same." So, at an early age we would go to business functions with my dad. We were expected to know who was there and to help with the entertainment. We understood that this was to make the magazine more successful. He never isolated business from home life. We understood that success comes from hard work, and he wanted us to see that at an early age—and to be a part of it too.

Dad enjoyed being with people and people sensed that. As a result, they were quickly at ease with him. He also was one of those rare individuals who never tried to make himself big by making others feel small. Perhaps most importantly, he was very generous with his time. Despite all of his obligations he always made the time for his family. When we did well, he took absolute delight in it. Dad saw life as a trip and he thought it was too short. But he believed that if you have a firm foundation of values and a sense of what the rules are, it can be a very good trip.

◆ Steve Forbes is the president and editor-in-chief of *Forbes Magazine*.

Mike Piazza

Catcher, New York Mets

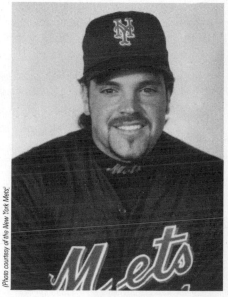

Mike Piazza

BESIDES BASEBALL, THE OTHER SPORT I played growing up was golf. In high school, I had several jobs during the summer. But just before my sophomore year, Dad let me stay home in August so that I could get ready for the golf team. One day we went out and played together. I was playing really poorly and I started to feel sorry for myself. Nothing made my dad madder than self-pity.

"Let's just pick up and go," he said. "You're not getting anything out of this."

I said, "Where are we going?" But he wouldn't have any of this. He was ticked off at me and my attitude.

"Look, let's just go," he said. "You're not working hard. You're just going through the motions. You're wasting your time and mine."

When we got home I was angry that we had left in the middle of the round. I didn't talk to my dad for three days. After I calmed down, I began to think about what my dad said and I realized that he was right. I really wasn't applying or focusing myself and I wasn't giving 100 percent. I was indeed wasting my time. That day at the golf course got me refocused and I ended up playing pretty well that golf season. That message that Dad taught me also applied to baseball.

Growing up, I think my dad, in some ways, believed in me more than I did. I was an all-state player for two years in high school, and my father was convinced that I wasn't that far behind some of the major-leaguers in terms of talent. But when I went off to the University of Miami, my career kind of came to a halt. I wasn't playing much and I felt my dream of playing in the big leagues was slowly slipping away. After my freshman year, I became really depressed. Dad tried to cheer me up and say everything was going to be alright. But for that whole summer I was in the doldrums.

"Stop feeling sorry for yourself," he finally said. "Life's not that bad."

Dad was always there with his constant, unconditional support and love. That was a big key to me. He got me out of my funk and then we became somewhat of a team. We tried to exhaust every avenue to get me some sort of exposure or opportunity to play professional baseball.

I transferred to a junior college to get playing time, but my luck there wasn't so good either. Although I got to play, I soon tore some ligaments in my hand. As a result, I missed the key time period when the major league ball clubs were out scouting players. My father, though, figured a way out of this roadblock. In the 1988 amateur draft, Tommy Lasorda had the Dodgers draft me in the last round as a favor to my dad. (Tommy and my dad grew up together in Norristown, Pennsylvania.) I was the 1,329th player drafted that year! Even though it wasn't the most glamorous way, I did get an opportunity to play professional baseball. Dad, of course, was so proud.

"Now you have an opportunity to play professional baseball," he said. "Don't look back. Look forward, and work as hard as you possibly can."

I took that advice to heart. Everyday in the minors, I was the first one out in the morning—working out with the coaches—and the last to leave when the sun would be going down. I definitely got my work ethic from my father. He was always adamant about having a goal and working towards it. He stressed to my brothers and me time and time again that there's no substitute for hard work and that we couldn't sit back and wait for things to happen. We had to make things happen.

When I was finally brought up to the majors, I felt like it was not only because of me, but also because of the emotional support I received from my family. It was a big plus for me to know that my dad supported me as much as he did. Life is hard enough for a kid, especially when you're in your late teens and you have your own insecurities about growing up and finding your own identity. But when you have a father who supports you the way my dad did, it makes all the difference in the world. His presence meant the world to me. Besides being my father, he's also a good friend.

◆ Mike Piazza is the all-star catcher for the New York Mets.

Elizabeth Dole

Former President, American Red Cross

MY DAD WAS A PERSON OF
incredibly strong principles and
that made an impression on me in
my formative years. I was about
three years old when we moved
into a new home that my father
had built. I decided on my own to
help decorate. I went around my
room and pasted thirteen
Valentines on the wall of this brand
new room. When Dad saw what I
had done, he wasn't very happy.

Being a disciplinarian, he took
me to each one and asked me,
"Who put these up?"

I blamed it on my imaginary
playmate, Denaw.

(Photo courtesy of the office of Elizabeth Dole)

Elizabeth Dole with her parents—Mary and John
Hanford—in front of Mount Vernon (circa 1970).

"No," he said, "he hasn't been
here today."

"My brother did it."

"No, Johnny would have put them way up high."

This went on until I had to say, "Liddy did it." After each admission I
was given a few pats with a broom straw switch that he got from the hedge
in our backyard. My punishment didn't hurt at all, but it certainly made
me feel terrible. I had disappointed my father. I loved and respected him
so much and I knew that I had really let him down. I learned a great lesson
in honesty that day and I never lied to him again.

My dad was also an exemplary manager of any and all affairs in
which he was involved, including, of course, his business. He owned a lot
of greenhouses in Salisbury, North Carolina, and he eventually developed

this business into the largest wholesaler of cut flowers and floral supplies in the Southeast.

As the business grew and expanded, he remained true to his values. They really were the hallmark of his life and his career. He was a man of absolute honesty, thoroughness, and industriousness. His word was his bond. You didn't need a contract with him. Everyone knew that whatever he said, he was going to do.

Dad was known for his loyalty to his employees and I think this really earned for him their true respect. Some of his employees worked with him for more than fifty years! During the war years when there was rationing, he was concerned about the people who lived in the apartments that he owned. Some of these families had children and he wanted to be sure that they had heating oil. So he shut down most of our house. That was his nature.

Mother always wanted my father to have a hobby or a sport because he was so immersed in business. She felt he ought to have something he could do with his buddies. So she persuaded him to try golf. One weekend afternoon, he was gone for a really long time. As the sun was setting, my mother thought, "Oh boy, he's really found something he loves."

When he finally came home he said, "Well Mary I played two games. . . ."

She thought that was great. He must have really enjoyed it. But then he continued speaking.

". . . my first and my last!"

For my dad, his family was his hobby. He had a loving marriage that lasted 60 years and he immersed himself in our lives. He was always supportive of anything that I did. When I ran for president of my high school, he was all for it. It was a very unusual thing for a girl to do, yet my dad was very supportive. And when I didn't make it, he picked me up. He said, "It's okay. There'll be another time."

I also remember back in my college days when he and Mother drove to Durham for graduation. The day before Commencement, we opened Duke's student newspaper and were quite surprised when we saw the front page. The *Chronicle* had named me their student leader of the year! Dad's reaction is unforgettable to me—he was so pleased and proud. He thought that was really special.

I think he would have been totally supportive of my run for president. He always said, "If it's worth doing, it's worth giving it your best." And Dad taught me by example. He was a very hard-working person who just gave his all to whatever he did.

After his death in 1981, I had to visit a number of apartment buildings he owned, whose construction he had supervised. In talking with their occupants, I discovered that their rents had been kept extraordinarily low. I also learned why. Some of the residents were widowed and most of them would have had to move if rents were raised. At least that's what my father feared. So that their lives wouldn't be disrupted, he simply carried them on his books.

The amazing thing about my father was that he never said anything about any of this. It was just done. Those were his principles. It was Dad's expression of a practical faith that regarded every man as his brother's keeper. That's the way he lived his life. I think a young person can't ask for anything more important than that—to be brought up with a person who had these strong values that were such an integral part of his life.

There's a Red Cross building in my home town and they named it the Hanford Dole Center—for my parents and for me. When I first looked at the blueprints of the building, I just thought about my father. It was the example that he set and the lessons that he taught that provided me with a blueprint for my life. He was such a wonderful father.

◆ Elizabeth Dole is a former U.S. cabinet secretary and president of the American Red Cross. In 1999, she became the first woman to seek the Republican presidential nomination.

G. Gordon Liddy

Radio Talk Show Host

I HAVE KNOWN PLENTY OF IMPRESSIVE PEOPLE IN MY LIFETIME. BUT MY ROLE model was my dad. He was a devoted father who was very much involved in the lives of his son and daughter. He taught us so much growing up— but perhaps most important was the true meaning of the word "loyalty."

My father was a very bright lawyer, but he stayed with a particular law firm many years longer than he should have. He certainly didn't remain there because of a lack of ambition. In fact, he was given many great opportunities to leave that law firm and go to others. But my dad refused to do so time and time again. Years later, my mother told me the reason why.

During the depression, my father's father was diagnosed with cancer and Dad didn't have the money to provide him with the proper medical care. Upon learning of my dad's predicament, the senior partner of his law firm made him an interest-free loan to pay for my grandfather's medical expenses. Dad never forgot that gesture. He was always very loyal to that man and it wasn't until this senior partner died, that my father moved on and started his own patent and trademark law firm on Wall Street.

Dad also taught me the value of hard work. I still remember the day that I learned to ride a two-wheeled bicycle. My best friend taught me on his bike one day after school. When I came home and proudly announced to my father that I had this wonderful achievement, he was duly impressed and congratulated me.

"I'm now ready for my own two-wheeler," I told him.

Without batting an eye, he looked right at me and said, "That's great. Now what job are you going to get to earn the money to buy one?"

I may have been young, but dad was serious. He taught us that if we wanted something badly enough, we just had to go out and work for it. Later that week, I went out and got a job as a bicycle mechanic. I soon earned enough money to buy sufficient parts to assemble a bicycle myself. That was my first bicycle. It never thereafter occurred to me to

ask my parents to give me
anything. I always figured that it
was my job to just go out and
earn it myself.

Sports were always a very
important thing with my dad. In
his youth, he was an avid baseball
player and was quite a track star.
He had a box full of medals and
he saw to it that I engaged in
sports. He would even take time
off from work to coach my team
in baseball.

I knew he was a fabulous
athlete in his day, but I once saw
a glimmer of his prowess
firsthand. One day in little league
our pitcher didn't show and
everybody thought we'd have to
forfeit. But my dad asked the
coach of the other team if it
would be okay if he pitched instead.
The other coach looked my dad

(Photo Credit: Ohio. Courtesy of G. Gordon Liddy)

G. Gordon Liddy with his dad, Sylvester James Liddy.

over—who was 56 years old at the time—and agreed. True enough, he got
tired in the seventh inning. But Dad simply took his glove off, put it on his
other hand, and pitched the remaining innings left-handed. He was
amazing. He just blew them away!

My father believed that education was enormously important. He was
the son of Irish immigrants—my grandmother on his side had an eighth-
grade education, and I'm not sure that my grandfather had much more. So
my father saw education as his ticket out. Even after the New York Giants
offered him a tryout in Florida when he was 18, he declined. He was very
grateful but he told them, "I am going to go to college and law school and
become a lawyer."

Dad was a brilliant guy and he put himself through law school by
teaching English. As a young boy, whenever I would make an error in

grammar or syntax, he would correct me immediately. And it stood me in good stead. I learned to write very well in the English language. My books have done quite well and I attribute a lot of that to him.

Dad's emphasis on education taught me to be the same way with respect to my own children. When I got out of prison, I was $346,000 in debt. But by borrowing money, getting a book contract, and through the use of scholarships, I was able to send three of my boys to private school. It may have been a stretch for us at that point, but my father taught me that's what you do for family.

When I refused to talk during the Watergate hearings, Dad was very proud of me. He knew I was doing what I believed to be right. And when he'd visit me in prison, he treated me with such dignity. You would never know that he wasn't visiting me at a country club!

The only time I saw my father cry was when I was a young man and I was getting ready to marry. We were just talking about life and he said, "You know, my father never hugged me and never told me that he loved me." There were tears in his eyes when he said this. This lack of affection, I think, always pained him and as a result, Dad frequently told me that he loved me. He would also try to hug me, but it was as if he didn't know how. I could sense his awkwardness and I've always remembered that. So, even to this day, I will walk up to my son—who's a 6-foot, 200-pound lieutenant commander in the Navy Seals—and give him a kiss and a huge bear hug. It never fails to embarrass the shit out of him!

Mrs. Liddy and I have five children and we've tried to instill in them those same values that my dad taught me. He was a fabulous person and a wonderful father.

◆ G. Gordon Liddy is a best-selling author and the host of a daily radio program that is syndicated nationally by Westwood One.

Kate Spade

Designer

I GREW UP IN KANSAS CITY, Missouri, and come from a pretty large family—I'm one of six children. My father is retired now, but growing up he owned a construction company that built roads and bridges. My dad's a pretty calm guy and one of the most patient people I have ever met. I guess you have to be patient to raise six kids!

He's also extremely confident. He's been that way my whole life. I, on the other hand, am the kind of person who worries a lot . . . about work and about life. But whenever I speak to my father and tell him in a frantic voice why I'm worried, he'll say in a soothing voice, "There's no reason to worry or to be nervous. Everything will work out fine. Things will fall into place as long as you're working as hard as you can." He's always had this calming effect upon me—especially when I'm completely falling apart!

(Photo courtesy of Kate Spade)

Kate Spade with her dad, Frank Brosnahan.

I've always loved fashion, but it's nothing I thought I was going to end up doing. However, I did always have the idea that I wanted a business. When I left my safe, secure job as an assistant in the fashion department at *Mademoiselle* to start up a new business, I think my father was nervous.

Still, he would never say that to me. Instead, he embraced my decision and offered me advice all along the way.

Dad always knew me to be quiet and never wanting to make a wave or be confrontational. As a result, he always told me, "Stay tough. Don't let them eat you up!" These pep talks gave me a lot of confidence as I was getting started. But I still didn't tell him the stories of the initial rejection we got. I know my dad, and I know how much he loves all of us. It would have upset him if he heard the many stories of being hung up on when I was pitching our fabrics to potential customers.

My dad has tried to teach me to approach life in a rational way. "Things happen," he'd say. A lot of times people want to say that something is responsible for it or somebody is responsible for it. But more often than not, that's not the case. I think that this approach to life is what kept Dad on such an even keel. He never overreacted to my successes or disappointments. He just kept everything in the proper perspective.

When we were just starting up the business, it was sometimes hard to get some customers to pay up or pay on time. Confrontation has never been my strong suit. So I called my father and asked him what to do and how to handle it. I have always felt comfortable talking to my dad about anything, especially business.

He'd say, "Get a Letter of Credit and if they refuse, drop them as an account."

He always gave me great advice and still made me feel like I was in control of the situation. But perhaps most important, he always had me make the decision.

The new company and the incredible publicity that we received excited my father a lot. He had people sending him articles from magazines like *Elle*. I wouldn't send them, however. I thought it might be seen as bragging, but Dad would have none of this.

He said, "Do you know how embarrassing it is to have a neighbor call me up and tell me about a magazine article about you?"

Eventually I got the message. Dad and Mom care about this stuff. I send them blurbs about the company or I let them know where they can find them. Dad gets very excited over this. You can absolutely hear it in his voice. He's really good about saying, "I am really, really proud of you." If he was really bowled over about something he'd call me by a nickname that he came up with. "Oh, my little Katnababen. Here she is—the businesswoman!" He's so cute and very sweet.

Dad's always been like that. I would play tennis with him when I was little and he was very encouraging. He was also like that in my school work. If I was doing poorly in one class, I worried about it and beat myself up over my inability to do well. But Dad would say, "Oh, you're doing so well in these other classes. Just do the best you can. Don't let it get you down." Dad always made me feel good about accomplishments and feel better about my disappointments. I have no doubt that my dad's instilling me with such confidence and a realistic view of life made it easier for me to leave *Mademoiselle* to start my own business. He taught me to be confident, but never cocky.

My parents divorced when I was eight, and I obviously spent more time with my mother because I lived with her. But the time that my father and I spent together was amazing. He always had this thing where he would take us on our birthdays to whatever restaurant we wanted to go to. Of course I would always choose someplace really nice! It was just me and Dad. I really enjoyed being with him one on one without the clan around. The divorce didn't mean that Dad dropped out of our lives. On the contrary. We still showed him report cards. He still came to all of my plays. He saw us whenever he got free time. So it was great having him around as much as we did.

I still remember going to the grocery store with him—he let us pick out whatever we wanted. I'd pick up one of those huge Hershey bars and I'd ask him, "What do you think?" He'd say, "Sure, whatever you want." I'd then look over at the Hostess Cupcakes and I'd ask him again, "What do you think?" And again he'd say, "Sure." It wasn't a very healthy shopping trip.

My dad was and is a role model for me—but not just in terms of business. Instead, I've always looked up to him and his values as a person. I have always admired his calm nature. It was just so reassuring. I never saw him overreact. It's a great quality to have.

◆ Kate Spade is a partner and chief designer at Kate Spade Inc., the handbag company she began in 1991. Through a partnership with Neiman Marcus, Kate Spade now markets everything from shoes to beauty products with Estée Lauder.

Michael Andretti

Professional Race Car Driver

MY FATHER STARTED RACING IN 1958 AND I WAS BORN FOUR YEARS LATER. SO my entire life has been around the race track. In the summer, we'd go out on the road with my dad. But as the school year approached, I would see my dad less frequently. The quality time, though, that we spent together was very special. Because he didn't have a nine-to-five job, when Dad was home, he really was home!

I learned much from my dad by just watching him. I saw the way he dealt with the pressures of his profession. He had many ups and downs throughout his career and I learned at an early age that this is a tough business. I also learned from my dad that everything in life balances out. For although Dad had a lot of bad luck in his career, he had plenty of good luck too. Dad taught me that if you keep putting yourself in the position to win a race, sooner or later the law of averages is going to work out.

I was never pushed into racing as a career. It was just something that I always wanted to do. So at the age of 16, my dad agreed to send me to about four different race driving schools—just to see how my ability measured up to other people. As it turned out, I had some natural ability and we decided that I should give racing a shot. And we decided to do it together.

As I started out on the circuit, having him there was a great advantage. I learned so much from him—not only about driving, but also about dealing with fans, handling the sponsors, and how to handle the crew.

One thing that took some getting used to, though, was the pressure. Having the last name "Andretti" often meant very high expectations, and I initially got caught up in the hype. In my first Indy car race in 1983, I had just turned 21. Dad qualified second and I qualified fourteenth. About one hundred miles into the race, Dad had moved up to second place and I was running at seventh. It was at that point that I looked up and said to myself, "Wow, there's Dad! This is big!" At that point my concentration went out and the next lap I spun! After the race, I told him what happened. Dad reacted as a father and as a mentor. "Don't let it happen again," he said.

One of my favorite moments with my dad took place at a race in Portland in 1986 on Father's Day. It was an unbelievable race. At one point

84

I was up almost two laps on my dad. The last 20 laps, though, I was having a problem with my fuel tank. So, I just coasted around the track, trying to save fuel. Dad kept charging hard. On the last turn of the last lap, my car finally picked up some fuel and the finish was basically a drag race. Dad ended up beating me by six inches in what was one of the closest finishes ever in the history of Indy car racing. I think it was the biggest Father's Day present Dad could ever get!

Dad's retired from racing now, but we're still as close as ever. We're in a lot of businesses together and Dad comes to many of my races. In the off-season, we actually live less than a quarter of a mile apart!

My dad taught me so much. But the biggest lesson I learned from him has allowed me to succeed in my career. Whenever I've come up short in a race or failed to achieve one of my goals, my father always knew the right thing to say. "Hey buddy," he'd say. "You made a mistake. Big deal. Just get them at the next race." My dad has always understood that mistakes happen and the most important thing is that I learn from them. Time and time again, he's given me the support that only a dad can give.

◆ Michael Andretti drives for the Newman/Haas Racing team on the CART FedEx Championship Series. He has won more races, led more laps, and won more pole positions than any other Active Champ or Indy Car driver.

(Photo Credit: David Taylor/Allsport. Courtesy of Newman/Haas Racing.)

Michael Andretti with his dad, Mario.

Jerry Della Femina

Chairman and CEO, Della Femina/Jeary and Partners

MY FATHER HAD AN INCREDIBLE WORK ETHIC. DAD WOULD WAKE UP EVERY morning at five o'clock to sell newspapers in the train stations. After rush hour, he would jump on the train and go to the *New York Times* and work in the composing room. He'd work there until 6:00 and was home by 7:00. And his day wasn't over yet! After dinner, he would then go out to Coney Island and run the rides until midnight. The purpose of this hectic schedule was to help the family and ensure that we had a better life than he did.

Dad is the eternal optimist. He always had a sense that things were going to get better. He had all of these jobs, but he never let his frustration or disappointment show. We didn't have that much money, but he was never envious of people who had more.

I learned much from my father just by watching his example. If I saw my father holding a door open for someone, I learned that you hold the door open for someone if they are older. If I saw my father helping someone out who was having a problem, I learned that you help someone out as often as you can. Kids are always observing their parents and I was always watching my daddy.

When I was about eight, I was with my dad in the subway when he found a wallet on the train. It didn't have much money in there—only about five or ten dollars. But as soon as we got home, Dad called the person whose wallet it was. He didn't make a big deal over returning this wallet. He just did it. Some lessons are never spoken.

What my dad showed me was consistency as a parent. He never flew off the handle. The best thing a child can live with is the knowledge that their parents will always be exactly the same one day after another. A bad day never changed his demeanor or his approach toward me.

I was always getting into trouble as a child. But my dad sensed that deep down I was a good kid. His reaction was always the same. "Don't worry," he said. "You'll do better."

Dad also never put any pressure on me to follow one path in life. He basically said, "You can be whatever you want to be." This was a wonderful environment for a child to grow up in. It left me free to pursue anything that I enjoyed.

My father is a very simple person from a time when things weren't that complex. He came from Naples with a core set of values: provide for your family, treat your wife well, and treat your family well. He also taught me lessons in gentleness and tolerance. I am very proud of my dad and although he probably never knew what a role model was, he was mine.

(Photo courtesy of Jerry Della Femina)

Jerry Della Femina

I called my mother every day for forty years, not because I was such a good son but because she was such a good mother. Now that she is gone, I miss her a great deal. But my father has filled much of that void. And every day I call him.

◆ Jerry Della Femina is chairman and CEO of Della Femina/Jeary and Partners, an advertising agency in New York City.

Joan Rivers

Comedienne

MY FATHER LOVED AMERICA. HE EMIGRATED FROM RUSSIA WHEN HE WAS A young boy and his is one of those great American success stories. Dad worked at night as a train conductor so he could go to college and medical school during the day. I don't think he ever slept! He saw this country as one in which anything was possible if you worked hard for it.

After medical school and a residency, Dad became a general practitioner. In fact, when I was growing up he had the largest GP practice in Brooklyn and Queens. He was a fabulous doctor who cared so much for his patients. My earliest memories are of spending my Sundays in a car as my father made house calls. That was part of the family tradition. While other doctors were playing golf on their day off, Dad used the time to make house calls. He truly was one of those great old-fashioned doctors.

Much to my mother's chagrin, my father never became a specialist. He loved his work and he loved his patients. The feeling was mutual. His patients would come to the office and they would wait for hours to see him. It was astonishing. They saw my dad as a healer and they just loved him.

Even though Dad worked so much, because of his generous nature money was always a problem. He often said to less-well-off patients, "Don't worry about the bill. You'll pay me later. The first priority is making you better."

Dad was also very sweet and funny with his patients. One time, my mom sat in the car waiting for him to come out from a house call. Apparently, he was talking loud enough for my mom to hear that he was talking to a female patient.

"Oh, darling," he said, "don't you worry." "Sweetheart, I am going to come around and take you to lunch and then we're going to go dancing."

My mom was furious—and jealous. She got out of the car and marched up to the house. When my dad answered the door, she saw the object of his "affection" in the living room. It was a 73-year-old little lady in a wheelchair!

Dad treated people with such warmth and such humanity. He made patients laugh—even on their deathbed. All my humor and all my sister's humor comes right from my father.

He also had a tremendous amount of compassion. To this day people come up to me and kiss my hands and say, "Your dad was with me when I had my baby," or "Your dad was with me when my wife died," or "Your dad was with me when my son's appendix burst." My father was an amazingly kind man. The only time I ever saw him cry was once when a patient died. He cared so much and saw his practice as an extended family.

I embarked on an entertainment career right after my graduation from Barnard. My father was very disappointed and that led to a period of estrangement between us. He didn't understand why I wanted to be an actress. It only made matters worse when every time a prostitute would come to his office she would tell him that she was an actress! He was hysterical! He should have looked at me and realized I wasn't going to make it as a prostitute!

Joan Rivers with her dad, Dr. Meyer C. Molinsky,

My first good job was with Second City in Chicago. I sent my parents tickets to come out and see me and I even paid for their hotel room. From then on, it was much smoother sailing. In the end, my father just loved every minute of my career. He'd actually carry clippings about me in his wallet! He also had 15 good years of watching me do my own Broadway play, host "Carson" and host my own shows. But that big bump in our relationship taught me something—you must let your child follow her own star.

My father never actually sat down and taught us anything. We just followed the example that he set. He treated people with such kindness. I think a lot of the good things that happened to me are because of the good things that my dad did for other people. He was a wonderful father.

◆ Joan Rivers is an Emmy Award–winning comedienne and the host of various specials on the E! Channel. In addition, she is the owner of her own line of jewelry.

Hank Aaron

Baseball Legend

I GREW UP IN MOBILE, ALABAMA, and I still remember how hard my father worked for the Alabama Dry Dock and Shipbuilding Company in order to support a family of eight.

My father always taught me to "do unto others as you would have them do unto you." He taught me the value of respecting other people—especially older people. I also learned a lot from the way he carried himself. He didn't necessarily say these lessons to me, but sometimes parents don't need to say anything. I could look at the expression on my father's face and

(Photo courtesy of Hank Aaron)

Hank Aaron

I'd know what was right and what was wrong. I think that's what you have to do with children.

My interest in baseball came at about 12 years old. Growing up in the South it was a different atmosphere and a different concept in life for black kids. There were no major league baseball players of color to look up to. As a result, my role models in life were my parents. Parents were role models to practically every black kid growing up in my day.

The things that I respected so much about my father were his values and that he wanted so much for his children. He stressed upon all of us the values of hard work, honesty, and respect for others. My father's words were always backed up with action. He was a very hard worker—leaving the house for the shipyard on some days at seven in the morning and coming back home around six in the evening. That work ethic was instilled in me. It taught me that no matter what it was in life, in order to be successful and if you want something bad enough, you had to work hard for it. That's why I always looked up to him as an icon.

We grew up in an atmosphere in which we believed in the Bible and the teachings of the Bible. Most of our lives was geared around that. The lessons learned in the Bible were the lessons that my father taught us at home.

I was blessed in that my father was able to see most of the milestones and highlights of my baseball career. He was there when I broke the home run record. He was there when I got my 3,000th base hit. I think in some ways it was more of a thrill for him when I achieved what I did. After all, I was the son and he was the father. He never had to tell me how proud he was of me. I'd hear it so often from other people to whom he had spoken. That's what made me feel so proud.

I have five kids but they're all grown now. I'd like to think that I instilled in my children the same values that my father instilled in me.

◆ Hank Aaron holds the Major League Baseball record for career home runs—755. He is a member of the Baseball Hall of Fame, the All-Century team, and is currently a senior vice president with the Atlanta Braves.

Howard Schultz

Chairman and CEO, Starbucks

I GREW UP IN BROOKLYN AND WAS raised in a working class family. We actually lived in federally subsidized housing. My dad was a high-school dropout and a war veteran who had a series of blue-collar type jobs throughout his life. He was a factory worker, a truck driver and cab driver, and never made more than $20,000 a year.

Despite the fact that my dad did not get paid a lot of money to do the jobs that he did, his work ethic was beyond reproach. His standard of ethics, honesty, accountability, and responsibility was exemplary, and he instilled those values in me.

(Photo: courtesy of Starbucks Coffee Company)

Howard Schultz

He also shared with me his love of sports, specifically baseball. Some of the best moments we had together growing up were at Yankee Stadium. We would either take the subway or drive up to the Bronx and sit in the stands on a Sunday afternoon. We'd talked about baseball, the Yankees, and what Joe Dimaggio represented to him. My dad responded to Joe Dimaggio not only as an athlete but also as a man. He loved Joe D. He was someone who had such high standards and a sense of grace and humanity that we miss so much in our society.

There were many days when my dad came home from 14-hour days of very physical labor and the first thing he did was look for me. We would put our gloves on, go outside, and have a catch. Those moments between a father and son are so special. Not a lot has to be said. But a certain bond develops from catching that ball from your father and throwing it back to him. Every single time I have a baseball catch with my son or my daughter—which is very frequently—the first vision I have is of my dad. I see a shadow or a glimmer of my father either next to or behind my son or my daughter.

When I was seven years old something happened to my father that changed the way I looked at life. I still remember walking into our apartment after school and seeing my father sprawled out on the couch with a full leg cast. Apparently, Dad slipped on some ice during a severe winter storm. He had been picking up and delivering cloth diapers—a job he complained about quite often.

As a result of the accident, Dad had to recuperate at home and we had to figure out how to make ends meet without any income coming in. Dad had no workmen's compensation and no health insurance. Our family was faced with severe financial problems. My father became extremely angry and disenchanted with what had taken place. That incident was a very powerful experience for me and my family. As I got older, it became the backdrop for the kind of company that I wanted to build. In many ways, I wanted to have the kind of company that my father never got the chance to work for.

There is a direct link to that incident and the values and culture at Starbucks. In the late '80s, Starbucks became the first company in America to provide comprehensive health care and equity in the form of stock options for even part-time workers. That, in large part, is due to what I experienced as a young child. My father had some bad luck in life. But everyone should have access to the American dream. I think success is best when it is shared. And our success as a company is directly linked to the fact that everyone has a chance to win.

I was the first person in my family to go to college and graduate. My father saw that and he saw the beginnings of my own ambition and perseverance. Unfortunately, one of the great tragedies in my own life is the fact that he passed on before any of the tremendous success of Starbucks was a reality. Not a day goes by when I don't think of him and think about how proud and joyful he would be to see how the values that he taught me have been incorporated into the culture of this company.

◆ Howard Schultz is the Chairman and CEO of Starbucks.

John Tesh

Grammy-Nominated Recording Artist

My dad was a World War II vet
and the way he parented was by
being very tough. When I was 14,
I told my dad that I didn't want
to play piano or be in the
marching band anymore. It was
the end of junior high and I just
didn't think it was cool. Dad
wasn't too pleased.

"Do you know how much
money we spent on these lessons?"
Dad screamed.

I was studying with a couple
of teachers from Julliard at the
time and was reasonably good.
But it just didn't do anything for
me with the girls. I wanted to
play lacrosse, football, and
basketball. Dad wouldn't hear any
of this. He made a plan where my
mom would stick this egg timer
on the piano for an hour and a
half every day while I practiced.
Dad even called my teachers to
make sure I didn't skip band. With
my dad, once I started something, I had to finish it and I couldn't start
anything else. As much as I begged and pleaded, he wouldn't let me quit.
He said, "Well if you want to play basketball and lacrosse, you still have
to go to band practice." Dad had this whole reward thing. As long as I

(Photo courtesy of John Tesh Productions)

John Tesh with his dad

kept my grades up and as long as I stayed in the marching band and played piano, I could play some of the sports that I really enjoyed.

Dad was also a big proponent of discipline. Both my parents grew up in the South and were into the whole spanking thing. When I acted up or disobeyed them, Dad would actually make me go out and cut my own switch for my spanking. I never viewed that as abuse. I respected my dad. I knew that my dad loved me because he showed up for everything. He was there for lacrosse. He was there for my football games. He was even in the front row at the concerts my rock 'n' roll band performed. He was very proud of my accomplishments.

My dad didn't constantly lecture me about this and that. A lot of times he wouldn't say anything. But I just knew that he supported me and cared. Every single night when I got home from school—two hours later—he would be there for dinner. When I was a boy scout, he'd come camping with our troop and freeze his butt off too. He didn't know much about camping, but he would just be there. I learned that's what's important about being a father.

As a teen, I desperately wanted to be a rock star and the only way to reach my goal I thought was to get a Hammond organ. The Hammond is a very expensive instrument and Dad wouldn't give me any money for it. What he wanted me to do was to earn it. He helped me get various jobs—starting a lemonade stand, cutting grass, and blowing snow out of driveways. He even had the idea that I should use my trumpet and get three friends and go around caroling for money on Christmas Eve! I'm an entrepreneur at heart and I think I got that from my dad. He instilled in me the idea that if I want something really bad, I've got to put in the work.

I can do a lot of things now because of my dad. In a way, I owe my career to his regimented ways. I hated the hard work that I had to do back then, but I think it instilled in me the incredible work ethic that I still have today.

Dad was about 55 years old and a vice president of the Haines Corporation when he just said, "I quit." He called a little family meeting and gathered us in the living room.

"I'm not happy anymore," he said. "I'm drinking on the train to and from work because I'm just totally miserable in this job."

Dad was a great fine arts painter and also a carpenter like you wouldn't believe. This is the work that he loved and wanted to pursue.

He said, "We're going to have to sell our house and move into an apartment. This is what I want to do and I hope you will support me."

My sisters had already moved out of the house for college so the move really wouldn't affect them. But my mom and I looked at each other in fear. We thought we were going to now starve to death! After I graduated from high school, we all moved to North Carolina—where it was cheaper to live—and Dad took on the work that he enjoyed so much. That courage and that risk that he took enabled me to leave that cushy job at *Entertainment Tonight* and pursue what I really wanted to do. My dad taught me that money doesn't matter as much as your happiness.

◆ John Tesh is a prolific musician/composer with 15 albums to his credit. The former host of *Entertainment Tonight* has won four Emmy Awards and received a Grammy nomination for his 1998 album, "Grand Passion."

Russell Maryland

Defensive End, Oakland Raiders

I GREW UP ON THE SOUTH SIDE OF CHICAGO AND WAS BLESSED TO HAVE SUCH a loving father. Dad worked for the Chrysler Corporation and was a pioneer, as far as blacks go, in the automobile business. He came up through the ranks in the 1970s and paved the way for other blacks in the automobile industry.

My father was always a hard worker and he never settled for anything less than perfect. He instilled in me and my two brothers a work ethic to finish whatever we started. Dad said, "Don't just finish it, do well at it."

Despite all of the hard work my father was putting in at Chrysler, he managed to attend almost every high school game that I played in. At times, he sacrificed some things in order to make it to my games. I might not ever see him arrive, but I could always hear him at the beginning of the first quarter! He'd be sitting up at the top of the stands being a father/coach. Every time I'd come from the field to the bench, I'd hear him yell in the background, "You've got to work harder, son!" It would be so embarrassing. But I realized there was a lot of love behind the yelling.

I can remember vividly when I received a scholarship offer from the University of Miami in the spring of 1986. It was my last year of high school. Dad was of course very proud of my accomplishment, but he also wanted to get me prepared for collegiate football. He felt I wasn't working all that hard. I, on the other hand, felt that I was doing much more than I needed to do as far as getting myself in shape and getting ready. But my dad had more foresight and knew it was going to be hard for me to adjust. After all, I was going to be moving from Chicago to South Florida, where the weather is unmerciful at times.

We were out in the park one day and after a full day of working out, he had the nerve to ask me to do some wind sprints! I was dripping in sweat and had been pushed to my limit. I said, "Haven't I done enough?" But he said matter-of-factly, "No, you haven't." It was the first time I was at odds with my father. But he wasn't having any of my complaining. I ended up doing those wind sprints and I even ended up doing much more than what he wanted me to.

But after going down to Miami and feeling that oppressive heat, I realized what my dad was trying to do. I still had a lot of work to do when I got to college, but thanks to my dad, I wasn't nearly as unprepared as I would have been.

My father would come to a lot of games when I was playing in Dallas. In fact, he'd come to so many games when I began in the league in 1991, that I had to say, "Dad, you don't have to come to every game!" But he didn't listen. That is until the 1993 season. That year he told me, "You're grown now, son. So I'm going to do as you say."

But my dad was there when I won all three Super Bowls with the Cowboys. I think it was a bigger deal for him than it was for me actually. I just looked at it as being another game. But he looked at it as being the most defining moment in his lifetime. In a sense, when I made it to the Super Bowl, he also made it to the Super Bowl.

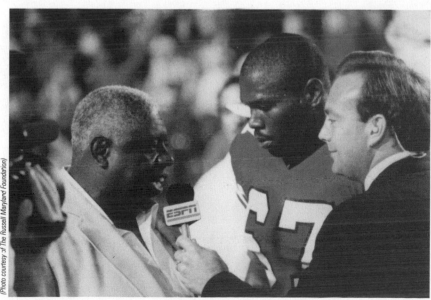

(Photo courtesy of The Russell Maryland Foundation)

Russell Maryland and his dad, James.

The thing that makes my dad a great father is that he always wants to see his sons going down the right path. A lot of times, in our teenage years, we thought we knew everything there was to know. But he'd always tell us, "I've been around. I've seen guys make mistakes. And I just don't want you guys to make those same mistakes." So he'd always try to do everything in his power to keep us on the straight and narrow.

My father forced me to play football as a 14-year-old when I really didn't want to do it. But I guess he saw some good things in store for me. And obviously after nine years in the NFL, I'm thankful to him for forcing me to play. We may not always see eye to eye, but I know that he'll always look out for my best interests. I know I can always go to my dad for advice or an honest opinion.

I often come across young people who tell me that I'm their hero. But when I was growing up, my father was my hero and my role model. A lot of kids these days don't have the opportunity to have a male role model in the home as I did. I had the blessing of having a father in the home who could correct me on a daily basis. He set the standard for what a man should be in our household.

◆ Russell Maryland is an All-Pro defensive tackle with the Oakland Raiders. He was a member of three Super Bowl champion teams.

Donald Trump

Developer

I HAD A WONDERFUL FATHER WHO
was a very strong guy. He was
strong in the sense that he was
very solid and worked very, very
hard. Growing up, he told me
many times, "The luckiest people
in the world were those that
worked the hardest." What he
meant was that to a certain extent,
you can create your own luck by
sheer will and work. But he also
said, "You need the innate ability
to accomplish your goals. Because
without innate ability, Jack
Nicklaus isn't going to be a great
golfer." My father instilled this
same work ethic into me.

My company has never been
bigger or stronger. But in the early
'90s, I was going through a very
rough patch. My father was 87
years old then, and he said, "Don't

Photo courtesy of Donald Trump)

Donald Trump and his dad, Fred.

worry about a thing. Just work hard. As long as you have your health and
you continue to work hard, you'll pull it through." He had total
confidence that I'd turn things around. That meant the world to me. It
inspired me to work even harder.

That situation was definitely a character-builder. I was billions of
dollars in debt and it seemed like every day I was getting hammered by
the press. But my father was a pillar of strength during that difficult
period. People would almost gleefully go up to my father and say, "Well,

Fred, it looks like Donald bit off more than he could chew." And my father would confidently say, "Do yourself a favor. Go back and bet the ranch on Donald."

My father wasn't just acting defensive. And this wasn't just bravado. He really thought it was stupid that people would even make such comments about me to him. He literally had no doubt about my abilities. The confidence that he had in me absolutely played a role in why I was able to come back much bigger and stronger than I ever was in the '80s.

During those difficult times, certain people unpleasantly surprised me. They weren't totally disloyal, but they weren't willing to go the extra step. I love loyalty and value loyalty and my father was a very loyal person. He had a group of people that he used for his building projects and he was always very loyal to them. Unless these contractors and subcontractors really let him down or did a bad job, he'd stay with those people. I do the same thing. If somebody did a great job for me in a previous building, I'll almost always go back to them for work on a new project. Because ultimately the quality of the contractor is more important than going with the lowest possible bid.

My father was also very compassionate to people who were having problems. Whenever he passed someone in the street that was in unfortunate circumstances and was down on their luck, he would give money—even if they weren't asking for it. He'd put his hand in his pocket and give them a $10 bill. I even saw him hand over a $100 bill once!

I learned a lot from my father from a business standpoint as well. I sat at his knee with building blocks when I was four years old, while he negotiated contracts for buildings in Brooklyn and Queens. Throughout my life, I learned about negotiation and about building by watching him.

One of the other things I learned from my father was that he loved what he was doing so much. He used to go out on Sundays and inspect a job. He truly loved it. And he taught me early on that if you don't love what you're doing, you can't be successful at it. You can never be successful at something you don't love.

◆ Donald Trump is a developer in New York City and president of The Trump Organization.

Chris Evert

Tennis Legend

MY FATHER WAS AN INCREDIBLY hard worker. Every day he taught tennis at the public courts in Fort Lauderdale from eight in the morning until six in the evening. Often he'd bring us down to his job to keep an eye on us and make sure that we were off the streets. Eventually he taught my two brothers, two sisters, and me how to play.

Growing up, I would be sidetracked sometimes with other sports or activities. I enjoyed tennis, but in junior high I wanted to try out for cheerleading. Dad never said I couldn't. Instead, he sat me down and explained to me how special my talent for tennis was.

"You can be good at a lot of things," he said. "But if you want to be great at something, you have to make sacrifices and then work hard at that one thing."

(Photo courtesy of Chris Evert)

Chris Evert and her dad, Jimmy.

That talk made me rethink my plans. From that moment on, I concentrated my efforts on tennis. Dad thought that having goals and working at something was good for us and would eventually pay off. Boy was he right! My achievements at a young age were an incentive for me to keep doing well. Dad provided further incentives for me along the way.

He said, "If you keep doing well and keep practicing then you can play more tournaments."

He assured me that any goal I had—whether it was the state tournament or nationals—was well within my reach. At the same time, my father always kept my feet on the ground. He allowed me—and encouraged me—to have a life outside of tennis. School was important. Family was important. And church was important. Back then, tennis was a part of my life, but it wasn't the dominant part.

If I lost a match, I would be kind of depressed the rest of the day. But once we got home, Dad would make sure that it was business as usual. We would set the table, have dinner, and maybe watch a movie on television. But the next day, we'd go back to the courts to see where we could improve. He was incredibly patient and taught me early on to deal with disappointment in a dignified way.

"If you lose, don't worry about it," he said. "You'll get them next time."

When I was on the Women's Tour, my father would help me to stay loose. He knew I was a pretty serious person, but he had the ability to get me to relax. He taught me to stay within myself and not to try shots that I didn't know how to hit. Because I traveled so much, often he'd give me that advice on the phone.

In my career, my dad taught me to think for myself. He instilled in me a tremendous amount of self-confidence.

Everyone always asks me, "Who did you have posters of on your wall when you were growing up?" The answer is nobody. My father was my role model. I have such respect for him and I don't think I am half the person he his.

I now teach my three children the same thing I learned from my dad: "If you want something, you have to work for it." This lesson applies to school, sports, or anything in life. If you want to be good at something, there are no short cuts.

◆ Chris Evert won 18 Grand Slam women's singles titles and is a member of the International Tennis Hall of Fame. She is a commentator for NBC Sports.

Julian Bond

Chairman, NAACP

I ALWAYS LOOKED UP TO MY
FATHER. He was an impressive
man who was involved in the
educational system my entire life.
From 1939–1945, he was the
president of a segregated state
school in Georgia called Fort
Valley State College. When I was
five, he became the president at
Lincoln University in
Pennsylvania. And in 1957, he
became the dean of the school of
education at Atlanta University.

Julian Bond

Despite this background,
education was not drummed into
us growing up. Instead, it was just
the accepted thing that we would
do well in school and that we would
go on to college. But even more importantly than that, because the number
of black people who had a college education then was relatively small, we
were taught that we had a responsibility to use our education for the
general uplift of the black race. My father said, "An education shouldn't be
pursued for its own sake. It has a much higher purpose."

After high school, I went to Morehouse College in Atlanta. I would
have been in the class of 1961. I say "would have been" because by my
senior year, I got caught up in the student sit-ins and the brand new
Student Nonviolence Coordinating Committee. It began to take up more
and more of my time. It also seemed more important than college. So in
the second semester of my senior year, to my father's great dismay, I
dropped out of college.

I lived at home after dropping out and I did what I could to bolster the Civil Rights movement. Mom and Dad were both angry and proud at my decision to leave school. They were angry that I would interrupt my education at all. But at the same time, they were proud that I was doing it for a cause that had swept up young people all over the South. Still, deep down, Dad was clearly disappointed.

I went back to school 10 years later and graduated in the class of 1971. My father got to see that just before he died. I still remember sitting on the stage and seeing my dad in the audience. He was just beaming! Like him and his father, I was now a college graduate. It was a great matter of pride to him that our family went from slavery to a third generation of children to receive college degrees.

All throughout my life, Dad stressed perseverance and hard work. My father used to tell me this one story all the time about this man who was hanging a picture in his house. He put a nail in the wall and it created a big crack. So he got a larger picture and he said, "That'll do." My father said to me, "Don't you ever be a 'that'll do' man." There are, of course, many times in life when you want to say, "Oh, sure, that'll do" or "That's good enough." But I always remembered that story and it made a very strong impression on me.

When we lived in Fort Valley—which was in rural Georgia—we used to go swimming and fishing in a nearby creek. I remember when I was four, I was swimming and I started to go under. My father, who was a fairly formal man in his appearance, was sitting on the bank of the creek in his suit and looking like a college president. As soon as he saw me struggling, he immediately jumped in and pulled me out. Well, of course, any father would have done that for his son. But I remember being tremendously impressed that he did this without any concern for himself. He didn't take off his shoes. He didn't take off his coat. He didn't take off his tie. He just dove right in. That day wasn't, by any means, unusual. Dad looked out for me his entire life.

◆ Julian Bond, one of the leaders of the Civil Rights movement, is the chairman of the NAACP. He also teaches history at American University and the University of Virginia.

Chris Elliott

Actor

My father was always involved in the entertainment business and had the type of job where I could go with him to work. And growing up, I did that a lot. Dad would just sit me in front of the cart machine and I would just spend hours with the sound effects radio carts. Whatever sound effect I wanted—door knocks, werewolf howls, or water dripping—I'd just pop in the cart. This just kept me occupied for hours!

By the time I was nine years old, I decided that I wanted to be an entertainer like my dad. I wanted to act like him and write like him. He worked very hard, but

(Photo Credit: Andrew Serrel. Courtesy of the Fox Broadcasting Company.)

Chris Elliott and his dad, Bob, on the set of the Fox television series, *Get a Life.*

he also managed to spend a lot of time at home. There were so many things about my father that I wanted to emulate.

When I chose not to go to college, my dad never questioned my decision. He was always very supportive and I think he always assumed that I would be the one in the family to go into show business. He saw how intense my desire was and told me I was making the right decision.

My first job was as a tour guide at Rockefeller Center. Just to get the job, I had to memorize a 75-page book and pass a test. Although I was never very good in school, I somehow managed to do that. When I was scheduled for my first day, I was extremely nervous. I was actually shaking. Suddenly, I looked to the rear of this group of 20 German tourists and I saw my dad! He never said anything. He just had this bemused look on his face. As I continued the tour and pointed to the skating rink, I saw the back of his trench coat as he walked away. It was one of those mysterious and goofy things that he would do. It was a pretty innocuous moment, but it made me laugh. I still laugh when I think about it today.

My dad eventually got me a job as a production assistant on a PBS show that he was working on. I worked there for a few months and then got an interview at NBC for what was going to be a new show with David Letterman. I was promised the job of visual coordinator, but when I went to the interview, they had already given that job away. All they had left was a job as a runner, which actually paid $50 a week less than what I was making at PBS. I was very upset and I told my dad that I wasn't going to take it.

"You're crazy," my dad said. "This is a great opportunity for you. It'll get your foot in the door. You can't not take this job!"

It was one of those rare times when my dad pretty much told me what to do. It could have been that he just wanted me out of the house! But he was also right. *Late Night with David Letterman* changed my life completely. I was a runner, then I was a production assistant and then I was a writer/performer. And all of that happened within a year. Had I not taken that job, I have no idea what I would be doing with my life.

The neat thing about my father is that he has never told me, "I told you so." There's very little ego with him. For somebody who's in show business, where ego is 50 to 90 percent of every personality, he's an anomaly. He's just so genuine. And he is so unbelievably proud of the success that I have achieved.

One of our most special times was when we got to work together on my own TV show, *Get a Life*. I was so happy that he got to not only see my success, but be with me for it. It was a thrill for both of us.

My father made a conscious choice to put his family ahead of his career. He certainly could have gone to Hollywood, but he decided to raise his family on the East Coast as normally as possible. Now that I have a family, I have made a similar choice. I love what I do and it can be very fun. But I also know that it's just a job. My dad put his family first and he taught me to do the same—a lesson for which I will always be grateful.

◆ Chris Elliott is a television and film actor who appeared in *There's Something About Mary* and starred in the Fox television series, *Get a Life*.

Rebecca Lobo

Forward, New York Liberty

OUR FAMILY HAS A STRONG FAITH and that definitely comes from my parents. There's also a strong sense of love in our family. I could tell—even when I was very young—just how much my mom and dad loved each other. I remember when we were kids, if one of them was going out, they gave each other a kiss good-bye. My brother and sister and I all thought this was really gross! But as I've gotten older I've watched them together and am amazed by how deep their love is. They never argued or fought—at least not in front of us. And they have always said to each other, "I love you." I'll never forget being in Italy one time with my basketball team and I caught a glimpse of them walking down the street holding hands. They looked like young lovers! I hope that when I finally get married I can find somebody that will love me as much as my dad loves my mom. It's just a great example that they set. I think that because there was always so much love in the family, I grew up being so secure in who I was and what I was going to become. I had this incredible security blanket around me that my parents provided.

(Photo courtesy of Ruthann Lobo)

Rebecca Lobo with her dad, Dennis Lobo.

My father is a high school social studies teacher and has been a track and field, cross-country coach for years. Growing up, we participated in all kinds of sports and our family also watched sports a lot on television. Our favorite teams were the Celtics, the Red Sox, and the New York Giants. Because we were so involved in athletics as a family, my love of sports came naturally. Dad never pressured us to play one sport over another. He was just always very supportive. Dad and Mom would come to all my games—something they still do today. Dad also got involved. If I asked my dad to play catch or shoot baskets with me outside, he would. And he never put limits on me because I was a girl. He never questioned my desire to play sports.

Both of my parents always encouraged us to follow our dreams. They would support whatever it was that we had a passion for. The only advice my dad would give is, "Work as hard as you can. And don't give anything but your best."

Dad taught me that you can have a sense of humor about practically anything. He used to make our lunches every day without fail. On my brother's lunch he would write a joke with a little cartoon on one side and the punchline on the back. Most of the time they were corny and not very funny, and I think he actually got more entertainment out of that than we ever could have! About a year ago I got a new fax machine and I wanted to test it and see if it worked. I called my dad and told him to send me something. Five minutes later a fax comes across the machine that had one of the old jokes that he used on my brother!

My mom battled breast cancer when I was in college. I was a junior at UConn when she was first diagnosed. The whole experience was particularly hard on my dad. Despite his anxiety about her illness, he was a pillar of strength for our family. Throughout her cancer treatment, he always asked how we were doing. He was always there for all of us.

He was also a rock of support for my mom. After she had a mastectomy, she never even considered having breast reconstruction surgery. My mom told me that Dad has never criticized her appearance. He never once told her to change her blouse and never once told her to change her hair. Instead he always just told her how beautiful she was. And that's why she thinks battling this disease wasn't as hard as it could have been. She knew that no matter what, he was going to be there and his love was going to be there.

Even now, when my mom goes away for a couple of days, he has a hard time with it. I think it's because it makes him think about what life would be like without my mom.

I don't know who said it originally, but my mom has passed it along— the greatest gift a father can give his children is to love their mother. My dad is a perfect example of that.

◆ Rebecca Lobo, a former College Player of the Year, is a forward with the WNBA's New York Liberty.

Robert Mondavi

Chairman, Robert Mondavi Winery

MY FATHER TAUGHT ME THE IMPORTANCE OF BEING COMPLETELY OPEN, completely honest, and laying all the cards on the table. He never liked conflicts. In fact, he hated to have any arguments. It was not his nature. If he had any differences of opinion with people, he would just quietly pull away without any fuss.

I remember one particular time when Dad and I were talking to a grape grower about buying some of his grapes. Some problem arose, and it became clear the grower was doing some double-dealing. I thought my father should pound the table or just do something to hold his own. But that wasn't Dad's style. He just stood up politely and walked away. I thought to myself, "My goodness, I'd be arguing like a son of a gun!" I slowly came to understand, though, that my father wanted to do business only with people he considered to be friends. And he always wanted to do business in an atmosphere of openness and mutual trust. If harsh words erupted, he'd just leave. Later, he might try to patch things up and restore harmony, and he was often successful. But if that didn't work, he'd just move on with his integrity and principles intact.

My father also conveyed to us lessons about knowing right from wrong. When I was nine years old, I saw some money on my father's dresser and I decided to help myself to a small loan. I took the money and spent it on candy. When my father discovered the money was missing, he was very upset. Boy did he get angry! I was scared pea green. I ran out of the house and he ran out after me. As I was running, I stumbled—and that's the only way he caught me! He brought me back to the house and I received from him my very first and very last whooping. Although that hurt, I learned the lesson. He made it clear—"You don't touch anything that is not yours. Always be open and honest." That was a big lesson for me and I've never forgotten that.

One of my proudest days was back in 1937 when I graduated from Stanford. It was also a very proud day for my father—a first-generation

American from Sassoferrato, Italy. Even though my father was running short of money in those early years, he saw to it that my brother Peter and I could attend this very prestigious and expensive university. That wasn't easy. When the Great Depression hit in 1929, Dad's grape and produce business hit the wall. We were in dire straits. But from nailing boxes in the summers, Peter and I saved up $15,000, which was a substantial sum back then. One day, my father swallowed his pride and came to us. He said he needed to borrow our savings. In exchange, he made us a solemn promise: "Once I'm back on my feet, I'll pay you back and put you both through college—any college you choose." As always, his word was as "good as gold." I wound up with two choices for college: U.C. Berkeley and Stanford. Berkeley

(Photo courtesy of Robert Mondavi)

Robert Mondavi with his dad, Cesare Mondavi. Taken on the occasion of Robert's graduation from Stanford University, 1937.

would have been cheaper, but I chose to go to Stanford and so did Peter. Dad kept his end of the bargain and paid our way. So even though things were tough for him in the '30s, Dad lived up to his commitments. That taught me to live by whatever commitments I would make in life.

When I graduated from Stanford, I went on my first business trip with my father. It was also the first time I had traveled alone with him. We left San Francisco by train and went to Chicago, and also on to New York and Boston. It was during this trip—by watching how he dealt with customers—that I finally came to understand why my father put his name,

C. Mondavi, on his business. For my father, business was not about money and negotiations. It was about people and it was about trust. A handshake was both a bond and a commitment. Dad did not bring along samples of his grapes to show his customers. He didn't need to because that was not what they were buying. What they were buying was my father's word. They were buying his expertise in California grapes and produce. And they were placing their confidence and money in his personal integrity. If the name C. Mondavi was on the label, that was good enough for his customers. His name and his word were as "good as gold."

My dad was a mentor to me throughout his entire life. He had really strong principles and was a visionary. Besides being a remarkable father, he was also a wonderful husband to my mother. I can only recall one argument that they ever had in my entire life. It happened when I was a young boy. And even that difference of opinion they tried to conceal from me by having their argument in the bathroom with the door closed! My father taught me to always be close with the family. "There can be honest differences in a family," he said, "but behind that there's always deep love." He also taught me a lot about generosity. He said, "The more that you give—as long as you're honest—it will come back to you in spades."

All you had to do was meet my father and you'd see how gentle and genuine he was. If my dad could see me today, he'd be amazed and proud at all that I have accomplished. I have not diverged at all from the principles that he instilled in me at a very young age.

◆ Robert Mondavi is the chairman of the board of Robert Mondavi and is considered to be one of the founders of California premium wine.

Brett Hull

Right Wing, Dallas Stars

WHEN I WAS SEVEN YEARS OLD, I never liked to go out on the ice and skate. Instead, I'd love to go out there in just my tennis shoes and walk around. I wouldn't let anyone put skates on me. Finally, one afternoon at one of my dad's practices with the Blackhawks, he and one of his teammates tied me down, strapped skates on my feet, and threw me all the way to the other end of the rink! Dad watched me go down and get up and go down and get up. And finally, I skated. I loved it! He couldn't get me off the ice—even when they turned the lights off! I think that very memorable

(Photo courtesy of the Dallas Stars)

Brett Hull

childhood incident says a lot about my dad. He felt that I had been coddled too much. He felt that now was the time that I learn to skate. He knew I'd love it once I tried it. Now of course it was something that he probably could have done in a much easier way, but it turned out he was right.

After I learned how to skate, I was never pushed into playing hockey. But what my dad did tell me as a kid was, "If you choose to do something, give it your all or don't do it at all." Commitment was always stressed upon me—whether it was baseball or hockey. Those were basically the two sports that I played as a kid. My father was very adamant about instilling me with certain basic values. He told me time and time again, "You don't go out there and do anything 'half-assed.' " This went for anything and everything—whether it was just throwing the ball in the yard or if I was playing in the play-offs of my little league baseball team. My dad taught me to go out and do things as hard as I can, to be the best and to win. I learned that there's no fooling around and there's no shortcuts.

When my father played home games, I doubt I missed a game. I actually got to sit on the bench quite a bit during the games. We'd also go to practices every chance we could. That was a great experience. I was able to skate with the pros and do things other kids never had a chance to do. Growing up, my father was my role model and my idol.

I was 13 when my parents got divorced. My father, who was playing for the Winnipeg Jets at the time, was getting near the end of his hockey career. After the divorce, I moved to Vancouver with my mom and didn't really see my father at all. But there was never any doubt in my mind that my father still loved me. And even though we didn't see a lot of each other, I never felt bitter about the divorce. I was smart enough to realize that my parents were not getting along and that I really had no chance of making them feel any different. I just knew that these things happen.

My dad and I never needed to patch anything up. We just needed to get back in contact. When I went away to play college hockey at the University of Minnesota at Duluth, he visited me quite often. And whenever he'd watch me play, he always pushed me to do better. He'd say, "You got one goal. That's great. But why didn't you get two?" He praised me when I competed, but he never let me get complacent with my performance. "You did alright. But you can do better," he'd say.

I also learned from my dad how to treat the fans. He always took time for autographs. He felt that's who his real audience was. He taught me the importance of the fans. Besides myself, my family, and my teammates, the only people I'm playing for are the people in the stands. I'm there to entertain them. Of course I have to do the things to help my team win. I've got to make a career for myself so I can support my family. But after that, I play for the fans. When people see me smiling on the ice and winking at the people in the stands, it's often misunderstood as nonchalance or not caring about the game. But, in between whistles, I'm there to entertain them. That's why I play the way I do. I love the offensive part of the game because that's what I think the fans enjoy.

Growing up as a "Hull," people always judged me by who my father is. They'd say, "How come you're not good? You're Bobby Hull's son."

And I realized when I was about 15 years old and was probably a "B" hockey player, that I'm Brett Hull and I'm never going to be Bobby Hull. It convinced me to develop a style of my own and play it as well as I could. Later when people would make the comparison, I'd say, "Yeah, I'm Bobby Hull's son. And I'm proud of it. But I'm Brett Hull and there's always going to be only one Bobby Hull." My dad's a Hall of Famer, but if I can carve a niche for myself somewhere or at least give it a try, I'll be fine. You can't fight those demons or they're going to be demons. You've just got to let it go.

Perhaps the best thing my dad instilled in me was my independence. He taught me to learn for myself, instead of having someone hold my hand and lead me through life.

I really think that as much as you need a loving family and a close-knit relationship with your parents, brothers, and sisters, it's important to give your kids freedom and independence and let them learn a lot on their own. That's the way my father raised me.

◆ Brett Hull, an eight-time NHL all-star, plays right wing for the Dallas Stars, the 1999 Stanley Cup Champions. Brett and his Hall of Fame father Bobby are the only father-son duo to each record 600 career goals

Abby Joseph Cohen

Chief Market Strategist, Goldman Sachs & Co.

M<small>Y FATHER WAS THE SWEETEST MAN</small> I'<small>VE EVER KNOWN.</small> H<small>E, OF COURSE, TOOK</small> pride in the successes that my sister and I achieved. But what made him so special was that he always took extreme joy and satisfaction in other people's success. And he would make sure that they knew. When I entered college, Dad became the first financial officer for *Essence*. He took such pride in watching this small, minority-owned business grow into such a successful venture over the years. It gave him an enormous amount of satisfaction.

Dad took this job after working his entire adult life as an auditor for a major accounting firm. And one of the things that he took absolute delight in was finding mistakes . . . and even finding possible fraud! Basically, he was looking at a dry set of books and he looked at it as a jigsaw puzzle. He took the time and effort to look at each puzzle piece and make sure it was fitting in the right way.

There's a good deal of that in what I do. I learned from him to never jump to conclusions and never take anything for granted. He also taught me that it is okay to have a different point of view—about politics, business, the stock market, or anything—as long as you thought it through and were comfortable with that judgment.

Dad was always very open about everything—not just work. Friends would sometimes say to him, "What's it like to work at *Essence*? Is it strange being a minority there?" And he always had the same reply, "People are people, and they're really good people." Dad was always nonjudgmental about other people. To my dad, people were viewed as individuals. He was always willing to think the best of other people and always willing to give them the benefit of the doubt.

My father gave me the same advice that he gave my sister and he gave my two daughters—always work hard. He didn't just talk about this, he demonstrated this his entire life. He went to college during the Great

Depression and accomplished this by working during the day and going to school at night. He then continued this pattern of work and school and got his master's degree before going into the Army for World War II.

He instilled this work ethic in me. If you expect to accomplish something, you really have to work at it. But perhaps more importantly, he also stressed to us that people aren't perfect. From time to time, there will be disappointments in life. The idea is to recognize that if things don't work out perfectly, pick yourself up and move on. Over a long lifetime, my dad never let his disappointments get him down. He just picked himself up, dusted himself off, and led a wonderful life.

◆ Abby Joseph Cohen is the Chief Market Strategist for Goldman Sachs & Co. Dubbed the "Prophet of Wall Street," Cohen has been rated the top portfolio strategist three years in a row by Institutional Investor's highly regarded survey.

(Photo courtesy of Abby Joseph Cohen)

Abby Joseph Cohen with her father, Raymond Joseph, and her sister, Sharyn Chanin (circa 1994).

Richard Branson

Chairman, Virgin Enterprises Ltd.

MY TWO YOUNGER SISTERS—LINDY AND VANESSA—AND I WERE BROUGHT UP IN a little village in the English countryside called Shamley Green. Our father was a struggling barrister and I always knew that he was special. He never criticized us growing up. Instead, he used praise to bring out the best in us. He used to say: "If you pour water on flowers, they flourish. If you don't give them water, they die."

I remember when I was a child, I said something unpleasant about somebody to my father. He explained to me, "Anytime that you say something unpleasant about somebody else, you should look at yourself. It's a reflection of you." He told me that if I go out and look for the best in people, I'll always get the best in return. In 25 years of writing notes to my staff, I've never criticized anyone. By praising people, you always bring out the best. People know when they've messed up. They don't need someone else to tell them. Like my father, I always look for the best in people.

Dad has also always been very understanding. The horrible English tradition of sending your children away to boarding school happened to me as well. I still remember the first night. I was eight years old at the time and another boy, who was the head of the dormitory, told me I had to get into his bed. I refused, and when I went back home to my parents that weekend, I told them what had happened. I remember my dad saying to me matter-of-factly, "It's best not to do that sort of thing." That's the way my father was. He never exploded in anger or called up the school. He simply dealt with things concerning me in a low-key way.

When I was 15 I started a magazine that would soon become a national magazine for young people. It was taking up a great deal of my time. Consequently, the headmaster at my school gave me a choice—I could either stay in school and do my school work or leave school and do my magazine. He wouldn't let me do both. After giving it a lot of consideration, I decided to leave school. I went home to tell my dad and we had a long talk as we walked around the garden. As any good dad would do, he tried to sway me out of my decision. But the moment he realized I had made up my mind, he leveled with me.

"Richard, when I was 23, I left university not knowing what it was I was going to do with my life," he said. "My dad persuaded me to go into law like him. And I've always regretted that decision. I wanted to be an archeologist, but I didn't pursue my dream. You're 15. You know what you want to do. You've got a dream. Go and fulfill that dream. If it doesn't work out, I'll do my best to get you back into a school again and get your education finished."

Dad always had a pretty understanding approach to things. He always gave me tremendous support. It was just fantastic. Ever since that day, every single adventure I've been on, my parents have been a part of it. Dad has been there for my boating trips and my ballooning trips. He's often looked after everybody in my family while I am away. He's done all this for me while having the added pressure of having a son who is constantly writing out his last will and testament while heading off around the world!

Dad also instilled me with the value of integrity. He taught me to conduct my life in a way in which I will always sleep well at night. I messed

(Photo courtesy of Virgin Management, LTD.)

Richard Branson with his dad, Ted.

up once as a teenager. I exported some records to Belgium and when I got to the Belgian coast I didn't have a visa to let me into the country. As a result, I had to drive these records back to England. Suddenly, I found myself in a position where I had a piece of paper that said I exported them. I realized that if I sold them in England, I wouldn't have to pay the tax. Needless to say, I foolishly sold them in England. This didn't go over well with the customs officials and I was soon arrested. For my father—the lawyer—this didn't look too good. Still, he supported me. He put up his house as security in case I couldn't pay the tax that was owed. In essence, Dad put his whole life on the line to make sure that nothing serious happened to me. My parents would have been kicked out of their house if I hadn't managed to work hard the next three years to pay off my bill to customs. It was fantastic what my father did for me. Ever since then, I've made absolutely certain of following his advice of doing things properly. He made clear to me the idea that your reputation is everything in life.

It's tremendous to be able to enjoy all my successes with my parents and I want them to stick around for a long, long time. One of the advantages of being wealthy is that I was able to bribe my dad into giving up smoking. When I offered him 20,000£ to give up smoking his pipe, he stopped in a second!

I've had a very happy marriage—20 years to the same woman. I've also got two beautiful children. And I'd like to think that we bring them up in a similar sort of way. There isn't one thing that I would change that I learned from my father. I'm just approaching 50 and it's great to still have my parents around and be able to share our lives with each other.

◆ Richard Branson is the chairman of Virgin Enterprises Ltd., a privately held international conglomerate, with $5 billion in annual revenues and 10,000 employees worldwide. Its businesses range from Virgin Atlantic Airlines, to Virgin Soda, to the Virgin Megastores.

Justin Leonard

PGA Golfer

THE GREATEST THING MY FATHER EVER DID FOR ME WAS TO ALLOW ME TO pursue my interests. He never pushed me in anything—even in golf. Instead, Dad always made me feel like I had some kind of hand in the decision making. He never said, "You need to go to the golf course and practice." Rather he would simply say, "Would you like to go?" My father left a lot of decisions up to me and then tried to support what I was doing. I think this approach allowed me to mature a little faster.

My father taught me to play golf when I was five. But he taught me so much more in terms of life lessons. I learned from him that you have to treat people with respect. The "Golden Rule" was very big with my dad. He instilled me with this value not only with words, but also with actions. I learned from his example. I saw the way he was with everyone—coworkers, friends, family, and strangers. This idea of respect didn't just apply to people. It also applied to the game of golf. Especially as I got older, Dad taught me time and time again to have respect for this game that I now make a living at.

My dad also taught me about the importance of trying my best. While he always was proud of my accomplishments, he also let me know when he was disappointed. I hated bringing him home bad report cards! Perhaps one of the most important virtues Dad instilled in me, though, was patience. Golf's a game that can be quite frustrating. But my father taught me the idea that things will come naturally and that there is no need to push them. In some way, my ability to concentrate and sink putts in tournaments stems from the lessons my dad taught me.

Dad and I played together this year for the first time at the AT&T Pebble Beach Pro-Am and we really had a ball. It was such a thrill to share with him what I do for a living. He was concerned about how I was playing and I was concerned about how he was playing. And if one of us had a bad hole or missed a shot, it was the other person whose head went down and felt terrible. It was a great day and I loved playing with him.

My father has worked very hard all of his life and finally retired last year. So it's nice to be able to see him finally relax. It's also great to be able to enjoy his company as much as I do and to have him come out to see so many tournaments.

While my dad was a great teacher to me growing up, he has become a great adviser to me and also a very close friend.

◆ Justin Leonard was a golf All-American at the University of Texas and won the 1997 British Open Championship. In 1999, his putt helped the United States defeat Europe and win back the Ryder Cup.

(Photo courtesy of Nancy Leonard)

Justin Leonard with his dad, Larry.

John Lewis

U. S. Representative, Georgia (D)

IN 1944, WHEN I WAS FOUR YEARS OLD, MY FATHER USED THE $300 THAT HE had saved from sharecropping to buy 110 acres of land in Troy, Alabama. He worked very hard and believed in what he called "making an earnest living." He worked from sunup to sundown—whether it was in the field or whether it was going into town to sell our produce. He even made the time to drive a school bus!

On the farm there were certain things we had to do every day without fail. If we didn't do these things or were lax in our duties, we risked losing the crop. As a young boy, I used to complain quite often about having to get up so early to harvest the fields and tend to our livestock. One day, my father took me aside and said, "Son, we have to do this in order to make things better. Hang in there and things will improve." Dad was an optimist by nature and he instilled in me this same concept of hope about the future.

My father would take risks in the hope of making our lives better. He planted new crops in previously unused farm land. He even began a corner grocery store that proved to be quite successful. Despite all of this focus on work, my brothers and sisters and I never felt neglected. We grew up in a very warm and loving environment.

Saturdays and Sundays were extra special days around the house. Dad felt strongly that we had to have a special meal on the weekends. He would go into town, buy some fresh fish, and even though it probably wasn't that healthy for us, we would have fried fish for Sunday morning breakfast. He felt that he owed it to the family to do something special. We would sit at the table along two long benches, say a prayer from the Bible, and then eat. It was a wonderful time.

Dad taught us in so many ways that we couldn't just be concerned about our own circumstances. We also had to be concerned about the circumstances of others. I saw my father always giving and always sharing.

In hindsight, this was remarkable in that we didn't have that much to share or to give.

Dad used to use this expression, "make do." He'd say, "We must use what we have and we must make do." He always had the faith and the belief that things would work out—even under the tremendously difficult conditions that confronted him. There was a lot of fear back then in Alabama. Segregation was very rigid. In those days, water fountains for us were marked "colored" and we could only walk on one side of the street. But somehow he survived these terrible circumstances without becoming bitter, angry, or hateful.

"Those are emotions that are too heavy to bear," he said. "And they tend to have a destructive effect on you."

I learned from my dad that you just can't carry around malice or ill feeling. It's very destructive and will eat away at your very soul.

Dad believed in being fair and being neighborly. He treated people the way he wished to be treated and saw goodness in all human beings. I never heard him say a bad word about anyone. Instead, he always gave people

(Photo courtesy of John Lewis)

John Lewis with his dad, Eddie, and his family.

the benefit of the doubt. He taught me that we all live in the larger community—together.

During the early days of the civil rights movement, my father kept his feelings about it to himself. I didn't initially tell him that I was involved in the sit-ins and attended the nonviolence workshops. It wasn't until I was arrested and got thrown in jail in Nashville that he knew about my involvement. My father was very concerned, but he never voiced any opinion against what I was doing. In fact, during that period, he became very supportive and extremely proud of my involvement. He would tell people, "That's my boy." He felt that I was doing something that he couldn't do, but something that should be done. This meant a great deal to me. It made me very happy to know that he was so supportive.

My father is a hero of mine. I don't understand how he did it. I don't think I would have been able to do what he did. Some people are amazed when I say that. They say, "You stood up to Bull Connor and Governor Wallace during the civil rights struggle. You were arrested. You were beaten. You went to jail." But my father was someone who brought 10 kids into the world very, very poor and did everything he knew how to make our lives better.

My father passed away in 1977. But if he had lived to see my election to Congress—from Georgia, no less—he would have been a very proud and happy father. I'd like to believe that he's looking down and watching me today.

◆ Congressman John Lewis represents the 5th District of Georgia in the U.S. House of Representatives. He was one of the leaders of the Civil Rights movement in the 1950s and 1960s.

Steve Kroft

Correspondent, *60 Minutes*

I GREW UP IN KOKOMO, INDIANA, WHERE MY FATHER HAD A NUMBER OF different jobs for Union Carbide. He started off as a supervisor in the foundry and ended up as a corporate vice president. He worked 40 years for the same company.

Growing up, Dad had that typical midwestern mentality. He worked very hard and he taught me to try hard at everything I did. He'd get very upset if he thought I wasn't giving 100 percent.

When I was about eight years old, my little league baseball coach yelled at me because I misplayed a ground ball. He took me out of the game and I impulsively quit the team. I didn't immediately tell my dad that I quit. But eventually, he caught on that I wasn't going to practice and he wanted to know why. He called the coach of the team over to the house and we talked through what happened. My father made it clear to me that he wasn't going to let me quit the team.

He said, "You never quit. You never give up. You just try hard and keep on working. But you're not a quitter."

That was a valuable lesson. He taught me to have a sense of responsibility for whatever project or activity I took on. He said, "You're responsible for your own actions. If you make a mistake, then you have to live with it."

When I was 16, Dad was offered a big job at Union Carbide's headquarters in New York City. It wasn't easy moving from a farm and factory town in Indiana to a snobby suburb of New York. Anytime you have to pick up and move and make new friends, it's very difficult. But this radical change in environment made the transition that much tougher.

My father was sensitive to our concerns of uprooting the family. He took my mother and me to New York so that we could check out the city before we made the move.

He said, "I want you to come out and see if you like it and tell me what you think."

When we arrived, we took a taxi into the city and went straight to his office building in the middle of Manhattan. We stayed in the Roosevelt Hotel, which was right near Grand Central Station. We went to a ball game at Yankee Stadium, went to dinner, walked all over New York, and, of course, did some of the touristy things. It was all very exciting.

My mother was much more reluctant to make the move than I was, but she never voiced her objections strongly. I accepted it as one of life's adventures. We both knew it was the opportunity of a lifetime for my father and something he wanted to do. That first visit to New York made me feel as if I was a part of the decision to make the move. It's quite possible that if my mother or I had said, "Look, we're not going to go," we wouldn't have gone.

Even though my father worked for a Fortune 500 company, he was always very supportive of my career choice—which tends to be a little less secure. I was terrible in math and I think he realized early on that I was not going to follow in his footsteps as a metallurgical engineer!

Steve Kroft with his dad, Frederick, and brother, Michael (circa 1959).

He always said, "You've got to find something that you want to do, that you enjoy."

After I graduated college in 1967, I got drafted the next year. It was a forgone conclusion that if I got drafted, I was going to go to Vietnam. There would have been no other alternative for me. This was mainly due to my father and what was expected of me. I think my parents would have disowned me if I went to Canada or went to jail!

While I went off to Vietnam, Dad continued to rise within his company. I think he became more attuned to the ways of the world and more polished with the time he spent at Union Carbide in New York. But the more successful he became in his career, the less time he spent at home. It was almost like I had two fathers. There was the father I remember growing up with in Kokomo, Indiana, and then there was the father I came to know as I got older who was a little bit more preoccupied and little bit harder to get time with. He had more pressure at that stage in life.

Now that I'm a father, I see how hard it is to balance work and family. I know that my dad did his best, but I would have liked to have spent more time with him. There are many areas where I'm exactly like my dad. But this is one of the few things where we differ. I'm trying my best to always be there for my five-year-old boy, John. This is the best lesson I learned from my dad.

◆ Steve Kroft is a correspondent for *60 Minutes* on CBS.

Kristine Lilly

Member, 1999 USA Women's World Cup Soccer Team

MY DAD IS AN INCREDIBLY TIRELESS PERSON. HE'S COMMUTED TO NEW YORK City from our home in Wilton, Connecticut, every day for 20 years. We live near the train tracks, so around dinnertime, I'd hear his train pull into the station. Two minutes later, I'd see him walk up the driveway. When he'd come home, he'd take his ten minutes to unwind and then he'd immediately be involved with my older brother or me. We'd play sports outside or we'd watch TV on the couch. He would leave his 12-hour day behind him and he'd focus on his family.

Weekends were also a big thing in our family. Whether we were doing sports, watching football games on TV, or doing yard work, we'd just be together. Growing up, we were his hobby. That's how he spent his spare time.

We weren't well off. But that never dictated what we could and couldn't do. It just meant that Mom and Dad often had to make adjustments in their lifestyle. They helped to make things work. I did horseback riding. I did gymnastics. I played tennis, baseball, and basketball. I even played the trumpet and piano. And of course I played soccer. Dad never forced anything. He just opened the doors to see what would happen.

My dad bonded with me through sports. Whenever he could, he'd come watch my games. He would be the typical dad on the sidelines.

"You need to score," he'd yell. Or, "You need to play more defense." All of this was done because he wanted me to be the best I could be.

Dad is not much of a talker, but I always knew he was there for me and loved me. He was incredibly supportive in everything I did, particularly in sports.

I didn't even know that the Women's National Soccer Team existed when I was playing soccer in high school. So when I made the team in my junior year, it was a bit overwhelming. I initially didn't want to go to the National Team camp or on an upcoming trip to China. I just didn't want to leave home. But my dad encouraged me and said, "This will probably be good for you." He didn't tell me to go, but he said this is an opportunity that I should probably take.

Since then, my dad hasn't missed one game of any World Cup I've played in. He went to China. He traveled to Sweden. And he saw every game in the United States. In the early days, before the huge crowds, I could even hear him yelling out for me from the stands.

One of the biggest losses I've experienced was during the World Cup in 1995 in Sweden. My whole family was there. After the game, everyone was upset. But when my dad saw me, he walked up and gave me a big hug. I think in some way, the loss may have been even tougher on my father than it was on me. As a parent, I think he tends to be very protective. He would never want my brother or me to feel any pain.

When games are really close, my dad just can't handle it. In our game against China in the World Cup, the game was decided on penalty kicks. This made my father a wreck. I was one of the kickers, and my father—I later learned—was freaking out when it was my turn in the penalty kicks.

(Photo courtesy of Kristine Lilly)

Kristine Lilly and her dad, Steve (circa 1999).

After the game, he told me, "I didn't watch it."

I said, "What!"

He explained, "I couldn't handle it. I couldn't watch it. I sat in my chair and covered my eyes. And when I heard the crowd cheer, I stood up."

To me that's my dad. His heart's in everything I do and he's so proud of all that I've accomplished.

Dad was the first member of my family I saw after the game. Our victory party was going on in the locker room. When I stepped out into the hallway for some fresh air, there he was. He gave me a big hug and just said, "I'm so proud of you." To me that's all that's ever needed. He's just awesome!

◆ Kristine Lilly, a member of the U.S. Women's National Soccer Team, scored one of the key penalty kicks in the U.S.'s win over China to capture the 1999 World Cup.

Yogi Berra

Baseball Legend

Dad was a very strict person, being from the old school. We always had work to do around the house on Saturdays. Each of my brothers and I had our own assignment. Someone had to clean the windows. Someone else had to clean the rugs. This was work we had to do. There were no excuses. But at four thirty, no matter what day it was, my dad would stand in front of the house and blow a whistle. That meant we had to drop whatever we were doing—whether it was chores or playing outside—get home, and get my dad a can of beer.

We were a real warm Italian family. Dinner was a real event in our house. It was a time for all of us to be together and talk about our day. Pop always got served first. And we never got up from the table until he got up.

My dad was also a man who instilled in us the value of honesty. When we went out at night, he would always ask us, "What time are you going to be home?" And I would say, "Well, I'll be home at nine." And he would immediately reply, "You better be home at nine!" And if you weren't, it was your butt. He always said, "You made the time. I didn't." We didn't have a telephone, so he counted on me to live up to my promise.

Even though we weren't that well-off growing up, Dad gave us everything we ever needed. (And when we worked, we always gave our check to Mom and Dad.) Anytime you needed clothes—pants, a shirt, a new suit, or shoes, Dad always said the same thing, "We'll get it for you."

My dad didn't like baseball. In fact, until my brothers and I started playing, he didn't even know anything about baseball. He came from the old country and his idea of work was the type of work that he did his entire life—hard, physical labor in a brickyard. He worked with his hands all day, working with a kiln making bricks. This is the type of work that he expected me and my brothers to do with our lives.

My older brothers were pretty good ball players too. And when they had a chance to go play the game of baseball professionally, Dad wouldn't let them. Baseball was foreign to my dad, who was an immigrant from Milan, Italy, and arrived in America by himself. He knew soccer, but I don't think he would have even approved of my brothers playing soccer professionally. He wasn't being mean. Instead, I think it was my father's way of looking out for the family. He believed in going to work where you knew where your next check was coming from.

(Photo courtesy of The Yogi Berra Museum and Learning Center)

Yogi Berra

As I was growing up, my skills as a baseball player grew tremendously. And as I was graduating from school, I had to make a decision about whether to pursue this game that I loved. My older brothers recognized my talents and they did all that they could to convince my dad to let me play. They said, "We're all working here in the brickyard. Why don't you give him a chance to play?" After thinking about it for a bit, he gave in. He told me that I could chase this dream I had to play in the big leagues. And he let me know that he was behind me. I'm glad that happened because I was quitting a lot of the jobs that I had back then. Dad would come home and see me and ask, "Why are you home so early?" I told him that they laid a bunch of us off!

After I made the big leagues, Dad was very proud of me and my success. He used to come out and watch me play all the time. That was great for him, but it also was a huge thrill for me. I loved my father very much.

Years later, I used to kid my dad. "Pop," I'd say, "do you realize that if you let all your sons play ball, you would have been a millionaire?" His reply was always the same: "Blame your mother!"

◆ Yogi Berra, a former all-star catcher with the New York Yankees, is a member of the Baseball Hall of Fame and was elected to baseball's All-Century Team.

Lou Dobbs

President and CEO, Space.com

I GREW UP IN CHILDRESS, TEXAS, A TOWN OF 8,000 ON THE OKLAHOMA border where Dad had a small farm machinery business. I worked on the farm hauling hay, picking potatoes, and doing other chores. But Dad always insisted that my schoolwork come first.

Dad may not have had much formal education—he left school in the eighth grade—but he possessed a world of knowledge. He was a voracious reader who could never get his hands on enough newspapers. He was smarter about current affairs than anyone I knew and I wanted to be just like him when I grew up.

He insisted that I take care of my schoolwork before I took care of anything else. When I worked during Harvest vacation, he insisted that I not work if I had schoolwork to be done—papers, research, whatever. I, of course, wanted to work because that was a source of considerable income to me as a young teenager. But he always put school first, even though we couldn't necessarily always afford doing that.

One thing my father could never tolerate was a person who didn't work hard. There was no nine to five approach. He felt that a person should give their all to whatever they were doing—whether it was schoolwork, chores, or their job. And I suppose I still have that bias to some degree.

Dad believed that praise was a more powerful motivator than criticism. He never once told me he was disappointed in me or that I should do better. If he wasn't pleased, his silence made it obvious and that stung more than any words. But when I brought home a good report card he would say, "Terrific work!" and that was enough to motivate me to bring home an even better one next time. This approach proved successful. When it came time for me to go to college, I was able to apply to some of the top schools in the country.

On an April morning Dad drove out to my high school in his pickup truck and asked that I be called out of class. Without saying a word he handed me an envelope that had arrived in the morning mail. Nervously, I opened it. "What does it say?" he asked. I was so excited I could barely form the words. "I'm going to Harvard!" I never saw Dad so proud as when I opened my first letter of acceptance.

Honesty was supremely important to Dad. Whether it was between a father and son, in the work world, or in the community, honesty was an integral part of his makeup. He stressed that an honest life was an honorable life. I always remember him telling me, "Say what you mean and mean what you say." Dad's advice was succinct. His actions spoke volumes.

(Photo courtesy of Lou Dobbs)

Lou Dobbs and his parents, Frank and Mae (circa 1938).

Dad has been gone 30 years now but he still lives on in me and my children. I tried to raise them as he raised me and I have wished countless times that he could see us now.

◆ Lou Dobbs is the President and CEO of Space.com. He formerly served as president of CNNfn and host of CNN's *Moneyline*.

Dick Gephardt

U.S. Representative, Missouri (D)

THE LESSONS I LEARNED FROM MY FATHER WERE MOSTLY BY HIS EXAMPLE. HE, of course, would talk to me about how important it was to be honest and to treat people fairly. But he also practiced what he preached.

I was 12 years old when my father went into the real estate business. (A bad back had forced him to give up his job as a milk truck driver.) On Sundays, I would sometimes go with my father to the open houses that he had. I saw firsthand how honest he was with people. When he'd have a buyer come into a house, he would tell them about the unnoticed or unseen problems. If the furnace didn't work properly, he'd tell them. If the neighborhood schools weren't the best, he'd tell them that as well. He treated prospective buyers in the same way he would have liked to be treated. I think the trust he built with people was very important.

When I was too young to read, my father read the newspaper to me every day. He'd read every section, but he would focus on two things—politics and baseball. Even though Dad was never involved personally in politics, he always respected the government and politicians. He would talk about issues and candidates, and when election day came around, he and Mom were always the first in line at the polls. As for baseball, Dad and I listened to every Cardinals game on the radio. Harry Carey's voice became as familiar to me as my dad's!

When I wasn't talking with my dad about baseball, I was playing baseball in the Boy Scouts. Dad taught me that participation in the sport, learning the rules, and playing by the rules was the important thing—and not whether we won or lost.

Because neither of my parents got through high school, they both saw the importance of education. In grade school, my principal called them in one day and said, "Your two sons could go to college. They have the ability and you ought to start saving money so they can do that."

After that conversation, they started saving their money religiously and helped us get together the resources for a college education. They had high expectations for us, and we were encouraged to learn and do well. They wanted their children to have a better life. Eventually, I went off to

Northwestern and my brother went off to Drake.

My dad was thrilled when we left home for college. But paying for our education wasn't easy. It wasn't a lot of money by today's standards, but for my parents it was an expensive proposition. Dad never complained though. He was totally focused on seeing us get a college education and was truly gratified when it happened.

When I decided to run for the Board of Aldermen in the city of St. Louis, Dad was so supportive—and involved! He went door to door with me in that campaign and also went door to door in my campaign for Congress. He was thrilled when we won. But he always told me, "Do your best. That's all that you can do." He made

(Photo courtesy of Dick Gephardt)

Dick Gephardt and his parents, Lou and Loreen, and brother, Don.

it clear to me that sometimes I may not win. But that's not what's important. To him, trying hard and playing fair were the most important things.

My father died before I ran for president in 1988. But my dad's hopes and dreams for me were different.

"I hope you're Speaker," he often told me.

He wanted me to be Speaker of the House. He thought that was the best job in the world. I'm sure that if he were here and I was able to do that, he would be very happy.

The most important thing in anybody's life is having the support of a parent. There's nothing that even comes close. I don't think anyone had as much impression or impact on me as my parents did. They were my most important role models.

◆ Congressman Dick Gephardt represents the 3rd District of Missouri and is the Minority Leader of the U.S. House of Representatives.

Terry Labonte

NASCAR driver

I CREDIT MY SUCCESS TO MY FATHER. HE WAS—FOR AS LONG AS I CAN remember—involved in race car driving. He never drove, but he was quite helpful to myself and my younger brother, Bobby. When we started racing, he built our cars and he built the engines. He did just about everything.

Driving was always something I wanted to do. I can remember when I was five years old, hanging out with my dad in his shop behind the house. Every night he and his friends would work on a race car in this shop, getting it ready for the races in Corpus Christi that weekend. In many ways, I liked Dad and his friends better than my friends. They were a lot more fun and they could do a lot more things than I could. We've always been buddies.

Dad got me started racing quarter midgets when I was seven, and I drove those until I was fifteen. We then built a stock car together and started racing it at the local track in Corpus Christi. From there, we went on to Houston and San Antonio. I raced two nights a week—with my father in the pit crew. It was a great experience traveling with my dad from town to town. Soon enough, I got an opportunity to drive Winston Cup cars.

I was 21 when I drove in my first Winston Cup race, finishing fourth at Darlington. It was a long way from the tracks in South Texas! It was a pretty big day for me and I think in some way it may have been even more exciting for my dad.

My father is a very competitive person. He told me many times growing up, "If you're going to do something, you do it the best you can. Never do anything half way." That's the way he is. He doesn't settle for anything less than 100 percent and he expects that attitude from everybody who's around him.

I played youth league football for a couple of years. One day, my friends and I were out on the field practicing and waiting for the coaches to show up.

My father's patience wore thin, so
he and another father just went
out on the field and became our
coaches. Dad was pretty
competitive at that too. I think he
got more penalties than our
football team did! He's just always
been like that. But I wouldn't want
him any other way.

When my dad wasn't pleased
about something, he let us know
it. He's not the type of guy to
keep it bottled up inside. We just
always knew where we stood with
Dad. He's a straight shooter who
taught us the difference between
right and wrong.

My brother and I still call
our father every Sunday night on
our way home from the races. If
he happened to watch the race on
television, we'll talk about what
he saw. If we ran well, he'll say
how proud he is of us. And if we
didn't run well, my father is always
ready with some advice and suggestions. He's a very smart guy.

(Photo courtesy of Labonte Racing, Inc.)

Terry Labonte and his parents, Bob and Martha.

Dad would always support us 100 percent in whatever we did.
This helped me so much as I set out on my goal of driving for the
Winston Cup. Bobby and I have been lucky enough to finish first and
second in some races and start first and second in others. It's really nice
that we get to compete on this level and our dad gets to see it. Back in
1984, my father was actually a crew member on my team when I won
the championship! It's such a thrill to see our dad's face after times
like these. All of those weekends back in Corpus Christi have paid off
in spades.

Today, our whole family lives in North Carolina and we're all pretty close. My 18-year-old son, Justin, is racing with my dad now, and I can't think of a better person for him to spend a Friday or Saturday night with. There's nobody better to look after him and make sure he's doing the right things.

Dad set a wonderful example and did a lot of things I took for granted. He provided a terrific home life for Bobby and me and I don't think he ever raised his voice to my mother. He's also been a big part of my racing career. If it wouldn't have been for the things that he did and the sacrifices that he made when I was racing back in Texas, it would have been a lot harder to get to where we are today.

◆ Terry Labonte is a driver for Hendrick Motorsports and is one of the leading drivers on the NASCAR Winston Cup Series. He is a two-time Winston Cup Series champion.

Alan Simpson

Former Senator, Wyoming (R)

POP WAS BORN IN A LOG CABIN IN JACKSON, WYOMING. LATER HE MOVED TO Cody, where I was born, not far from Yellowstone National Park. We would return to Jackson for summer vacations and these are my happiest memories: fishing for cutthroat trout in the Snake River, climbing mountains, frying steaks over a campfire, and singing goofy songs.

Professionally, Pop was a lawyer. But much of his time was spent with civic organizations—the American Legion, the Lions, Rotary, his Masonic Order, you name it. Even with such a busy schedule, he always made time for family.

Pop was a fierce competitor who used to say, "Show me a good loser and I'll show you a loser." He wasn't telling me to be a bad sport. He was urging me not to accept anything short of my best effort. When I was nine, Pop decided to run for the U.S. Senate. He was wiped out by a popular Democratic incumbent and went into a funk like I had never seen. One of the first things he did was cancel lots of magazine subscriptions. He used to read everything to keep up on politics, but in the wake of this disappointing loss, he saw no use for them.

After a few weeks, though, he started to bounce back. He admitted, "Any damn fool can be unhappy. Hatred corrodes the container it's carried in." Pop made me realize that it does no good to blame others when you are down. As he used to say, "It's your own damn fault."

That was Pop's philosophy: take responsibility for your actions. I learned this the hard way. In high school, I was known as "Alibi Al" because I tried to get away with everything and was usually successful. But when I was 18 I was arrested for shooting up mailboxes with a shotgun and was placed on federal probation for two years.

Mother was devastated, but Pop never said anything. Six months later we were all sitting at dinner and somehow the subject came up. Then Pop did something I had never seen before and never saw again. He started crying. "Where have we failed?" he asked.

I was devastated. I had disappointed to the point of tears the man I loved and admired more than anyone else in the world. Up until that point in my life I hadn't taken anything seriously. I weighed 260 pounds and thought beer was food. But on that day I started to grow up. I realized for the first time that actions have consequences and that mine had embarrassed the entire family. I vowed it would never happen again.

Fortunately my actions did not completely ruin Pop's reputation. In 1954, when I was 23, he was elected governor of Wyoming. After two terms he ran for that Senate seat and won.

Pop's positive outlook was crucial to his success, and mine. As I followed in his footsteps I strived to live up to his example. Pop taught me that feelings of gloom and doom, hatred, or jealousy have no place in a productive life and that you should always strive to improve. As Pop would say, "Don't sit on your ass and bark at the moon. Get in the game!" Boy, was he ever right!

◆ Alan K. Simpson (R, Wyoming) retired from the U.S. Senate in 1996 after serving three terms. He is now the director of the Institute of Politics at Harvard University's John F. Kennedy School of Government.

(Photo courtesy of Alan Simpson)

Alan Simpson and his father, Milward (and some family friends). (circa 1958).

Christine Todd Whitman

Governor of New Jersey

ONE OF THE GUIDING PRINCIPLES IN my father's life was, "Anything worth doing was worth doing well." He applied this lesson to everything my older sister, my brothers, and I did. I still remember when I was about seven, we were out West for a family vacation at a ranch in Wyoming, and my father wanted me to go fly-fishing with him. All the other kids were out riding horses, playing softball, or playing games, and he made me stand in front of our cabin casting a fishing line. I was not a happy camper. But his attitude was that if I was going to go out fishing with him—which I desperately wanted to do—he wanted me to really be able to fish well. He was very strict and demanding in that way.

It wasn't until about 10 or 15 years later when I was thinking about it that I came to realize that he did that because he really loved

(Photo courtesy of Christine Todd Whitman)

Christine Todd Whitman and her dad, Webster B. Todd.

me. He wanted me to go out and have a good time with him, and he knew that I wasn't going to have a good time if I didn't know what I was doing. I would have been spending my entire time untangling my fly from the bush behind me. This fit in so perfectly with his overall attitude—that you owe it to yourself and others to do the very best you can in any endeavor. It didn't mean that I had to win every time in an athletic contest. It also didn't mean that I had to get A's in school all the time. The point was—you have to try. "You don't succeed at anything if you don't try," he'd tell me time and time again. Sometimes it was a little harsh and a little demanding and you rebel against it, but over time as I look back, I am very thankful for having had that kind of a role model.

Dad also instilled in me his firm belief that your word is your bond. He was one of the most honest people I think I have ever met. When I was growing up, he served as New Jersey's Republican State chairman. Yet he was one of those people who was admired and respected by both sides of the aisle. People knew they could talk to him and the conversation would remain private. They also knew that if he made a deal, it was a deal they could count on and there was never anything in it for him.

He and my mother put a very high premium on telling the truth. If Dad felt someone wasn't being forthright or wasn't trustworthy, that person would never be high in his esteem. And if people went back on their word, it was something that upset him and caused him a lot of concern. He didn't treat people that way, so he was always surprised by it when it happened to him. "Honesty," he said, "tells people a lot about who you are and what you are."

Dad also felt very strongly that if you cared about the system, you had to be involved. You couldn't just sit back. Dad had no time for people who just complained but would not bother to vote, not bother to go to meetings, and not bother to stay involved except when they were mad about something. He taught me to look at politics and government as a way to make a difference. He believed in the process. He strongly supported our system of government.

I also learned from my dad what true leadership is. He taught me that in politics everybody is not going to support me in everything I do. "What's important," he said, "is that you stick to your core values." If people don't support you, then so be it. It goes back to being true to yourself.

Dad died in 1989. He was alive when I first ran for freeholder, but I would have loved to have him around while serving as governor. He taught me so much about public service and about life.

◆ Christine Todd Whitman is serving her second term as governor of New Jersey.

J.C. Watts

U. S. Representative, Oklahoma (R)

OUTSIDE OF MY RELATIONSHIP WITH CHRIST, MY FATHER IS THE ONE PERSON who has had the most influence on my life. One of the great lessons that I picked up from my father was that hard work is a virtue. He always talked about hard work, sacrifice, and commitment. And I saw him living those same principles.

I never remember him having fewer than two jobs the whole time I grew up under his roof. His routine for years was unbelievable. He'd go to work as a policeman from about ten at night to seven in the morning. He'd get off and then sleep for two and a half hours. He'd wake up and then farm until about five in the evening. Then he'd bathe, eat dinner, watch the evening news, go to sleep from about 6 P.M. to 9 P.M. and then get ready for work all over again. On the weekends, he added another job to his busy schedule—minister.

He had six kids and we may not have appreciated his philosophy from time to time. But I think hard work is the one value that every one of my brothers and sisters and I learned from him. I spent a lot of time working with him growing up—hauling hay or helping to move people—and from time to time he'd talk to me about his philosophy of life: "Hard work never killed anybody."

In the summer, we would plant gardens in the morning. Those garden rows would seem like they were a mile long! I'd get out there with the hoe and boy was it boring, tedious, and hot! But you did it—no questions asked. All day long we'd pick okra or cucumber, feed the chickens and hogs, or chop the potatoes. It didn't matter if you came in at two o'clock in the morning. At six in the morning, you'd better be up when Daddy got up and raring to go. That was just expected. I may not have liked it, but it was what I had to do.

Two days in the seventh grade is the extent of my dad's education. He never preached to me on a daily basis that I had to go to school. But it was clear that he wanted all of us to better ourselves and get an education. You just knew that you didn't want the wrath of Buddy Watts on you because you were playing hooky or you were tardy. You just did what was right. My daddy stressed to me that not only was I going to go to school, but I was going to act civilized once I got there.

My dad's generation wasn't apt to express themselves that often. My father didn't make a big fuss about things you should be doing. It was just expected. He had that Nike attitude long before Nike came along—"Just Do It."

I remember when I first went off to college at the University of Oklahoma—I quit twice my freshman year. I literally packed my bags and went home. The first time I was a little homesick and really was a bit overwhelmed by this huge campus. But I went back with the attitude that I'm going to give this college thing one more shot.

The second time I came back home, Daddy had a different attitude. My coach, Barry Switzer, had already called my dad at home. So Daddy knew to expect me when I came through the front door. He was always patient with me and I have always valued his advice. As I unpacked my clothes, he came into my room and gave me one of those stares you never forget. After what seemed like ten minutes, he said, "Well I'm

(Photo courtesy of Christine Todd Whitman)

J.C. Watts and his dad, Buddy Watts (circa 1991).

not going to try to influence you one way or the other. Whether to quit or go back to school—it's a decision you've got to make on your own. You're old enough to make that decision on your own. But you need to realize that if what you're doing were easy, everybody would be doing it."

Daddy saying that to me meant a lot. I came to understand his sacrifices throughout my life. He never quit and he never let me down. He caught me at the right point and it resonated with me. That evening, I packed my bags up again—this time to go back to campus in Norman.

Everything that my father accomplished in life, he accomplished by a strong faith, common sense, and hard work. These were the assets that my father built and made a living on. To this day—at 75 years of age—he still gets on his tractor and still gets on top of the house to fix the roof. He still puts in quite a hard day's work after two heart surgeries. He made me believe from an early age that I could accomplish anything that I wanted to accomplish as long as I wasn't afraid to work hard.

◆ Congressman J.C. Watts represents the 4th District of Oklahoma and is the chairman of the House Republican Conference. He is the highest ranking African-American in the Republican party.

Tori Spelling

Actor

I HAVE ALWAYS BEEN A DADDY'S GIRL. IT MAY SEEM OBVIOUS, BUT MY DAD HAS been such an important part of my life and such an important part of my career. Although my dad was very well known and respected in the entertainment business, he never pushed me into acting. It was just something I always wanted to do. And whether it was school or acting, my dad was always behind me 100 percent. From an early age, Dad would say to me, "Do whatever you believe in and make sure you love what you do." That's the secret to his success as a television producer. He loves what he does.

When I was five, I told my dad that I wanted to act. He immediately found ways to help me out. He gave me little guest star parts in some of the shows that he produced. He encouraged me to act in plays at school (and he came to every one of them). Even when he would get home at eight o'clock at night after a very long day at work, he would help me prepare for auditions. He would work with me for about two hours, and we would go over it again and again. He'd say, "Try reading it this way. See how it comes out."

He had this word that he made up and whenever he thought I nailed the reading, he would say "Baby, that was just right, that was plu-perfect." I said, "Plu-perfect?" And he said, "Yep, that's better than perfect, that's plu-perfect." I would just beam. That was all that mattered . . . whether he liked it or not.

What was amazing about my dad was how hard he worked. He had about 13 shows on the air at the same time, including *Fantasy Island, The Love Boat, Dynasty, Hotel,* and *T. J. Hooker.* And yet despite all of his obligations, he always made time for my brother, my mom, and me.

As I set off on my own career, Dad weighed all of my options with me. He told me to believe in myself and my abilities. And he taught me how to handle success and how to deal with failure. Dad said, "If acting doesn't work out or you decide you don't want to do it, that's fine. Whatever happens, happens." Hearing those words meant a lot. I knew my dad loved me unconditionally, but he took a lot of pressure off of me and made me feel that I could do it. He managed to do all of this without treating me like a child. That's the great thing about my dad—he always talked to me like we were on the same level.

(Photo courtesy of the Fox Broadcasting Company)

Tori Spelling

My brother and I grew up in very fortunate circumstances. But my dad taught us from an early age to really appreciate what we have and to treat everybody the same. "Having money doesn't exempt you from anything," he said. "You still have to work very hard and believe in yourself."

My dad is an inspiration to a lot of people. He came from nothing and yet he has achieved so much. He is, without a doubt, the most creative person I have ever known. I have so much respect for him on that level. But growing up, I never saw him as this huge mogul. I just see him as a wonderful father who gives me good advice about everything and makes me feel good about myself. He's not only the best father I could ever ask for, he's also a great friend.

◆ Tori Spelling is a television and film actor. She is one of the original cast members of the Fox TV series, *Beverly Hills 90210*.

Richard Holbrooke

U.S. Ambassador to the United Nations

MY FATHER WAS A REFUGEE FROM STALINIST RUSSIA WHO ARRIVED IN THE United States in 1938. He loved America and was incredibly grateful for the benefits and the opportunities that this country had given him.

After completing his medical training in New York, Dad became an amazingly compassionate physician. He made house calls and actually listed our home phone number. This led to quite a few phone calls to our house in the middle of the night! Dad never complained, though. He said it was his responsibility.

My father was a very gentle person—and not just with his patients. When I was 10 years old, he found a wounded bird in our backyard in Scarsdale that clearly was not going to survive. Still, Dad tried to keep it alive by giving it an injection of adrenaline. When this failed and the bird died, Dad insisted on giving it a formal burial. He believed very much in the sanctity of life. He had seen war and destruction in Europe and I think this experience affected him very greatly.

We had many philosophical discussions growing up. We often debated about the limits of pacifism and other serious topics. We may have disagreed sometimes, but he taught me to have a willingness to listen to anybody on any side of any issue and try to have an empirical approach to dealing with problems. "Events impact on each other in unpredictable ways," he'd say. "And one has to be open to a new dynamic."

His most enduring gift to me was intellectual curiosity. My father taught me to be open to all possibilities. But I also learned not to accept something as given simply because some person in authority says it is true. He felt that everything needs to be demonstrated empirically.

He deeply believed in science and wanted me to be a nuclear physicist. If you grew up in the late 1940s, the gigantic figures were not necessarily Truman or Acheson or even George Marshall, whom we celebrate today. They were Einstein and Oppenheimer, who had looked into the mysteries of the universe. These scientists were fantastic figures. Dad would have never dreamed that I would end up doing what I am doing today. But I do not think that he would be unhappy about it. He valued peace and respected anyone who could help settle conflicts, reduce tensions, or help other human beings.

The other thing he taught me is that "Even your adversary has a point of view." That doesn't mean the other person has an equally valid point of view. But I learned from my father that even when you are dealing with somebody you totally disagree with, you have to try to figure out what it is that drives him.

Dad was enormously proud of the things that I did. I was the sports editor of my high school newspaper and also wrote articles about the baseball team for the *Scarsdale Inquirer*. Dad clipped every article I wrote! He was also totally possessed with the American dream and of its potential. In the summer of 1956, my parents decided that I should go away for the summer because my father was very ill. They sent me to stay with a French family in the Loire Valley. The head of the family was a doctor who went to medical school with my father. At the end of the summer, Dr. Cartienne wrote a letter to my parents, which they were very proud of. In it, he wrote: "Your son is 100 percent American." That sentence was an affirmation of everything my father hoped for.

(Photo courtesy of the U.S. Mission to the United Nations)

Ambassador Richard Holbrooke

When my youngest son, Anthony, was in Thailand registering refugees to see which ones were eligible to come to the United States, he wrote me an amazing letter in which he said, "It just occurred to me that I am the grandson of refugees, my father has worked with refugees all his life, and here I am on the Cambodian border helping refugees." I sent that letter to my mother and she was immensely touched by it. My children possess that same openness that my father had.

Nothing is more important than one's father to a son. He taught me so much, but my greatest regret is that I was so young when he died.

◆ Richard Holbrooke is the U.S. ambassador to the United Nations. He formerly served as an assistant secretary of state and was the principle architect of the Dayton Peace Accords that ended the war in Bosnia in late 1995.

Kevin Stocker

Shortstop, Tampa Bay Devil Rays

I COME FROM A VERY ATHLETIC FAMILY. MY OLDER BROTHERS PLAYED baseball. My twin sister was a Washington State gymnastics and track champion. And I played everything—basketball, baseball, football, and golf. I even bowled! When Dad wasn't serving as our coach, he was always there watching and encouraging everything that we did.

Growing up, I was a little hothead. It was quite common for me to act up. In seventh grade, I played in a basketball game that was definitely not my best performance—either as a player or as a young man. I received two technical fouls—once for kicking the wall after missing a lay-up; the other one was for saying a few profanities.

Dad, who was a school superintendent, was at the gym that day and he saw my behavior. He had seen me act up on the court and on the field before. But this was different. I was 13, and these incidents were clearly becoming an old story. On this afternoon, Dad sort of kept his own anger inside. He didn't say anything to me at school, but when I got home he let me have it. He was not very pleased with my attitude. He said, "When you're on the court, you not only represent yourself, you also represent your teammates and your school." It was a rare occasion when my dad lit into me. In our home, you'd have to do something pretty bad to get chewed out by my dad. This affected me greatly. It may have been a scare tactic, but it sure worked. Ever since then, I've really straightened up my act.

Most often though, Dad was there for encouragement. He used to come home from working all day long and he'd say, "Let's go out and throw the baseball." We'd go in the backyard and he'd mark the distance for what a little league mound is to home plate. He would then sit out there catching for almost two hours. He'd give me instruction, we'd talk about my day at school, and we'd laugh over some corny joke I recently heard. I respected my dad. The reason why he had such an impact on me and my brothers and sister was that he didn't treat us like we were babies. He let us find things out for ourselves. And sometimes these were hard lessons.

When I was 16 and had just finished taking my SATs, I got into an accident as I drove home from school with my sister and three friends. It was clearly my fault. To make matters worse, this wasn't just any car I had banged up. It was my dad's new car! The tow truck operator took one look at the front of the car and gave me the bad news—it was totaled. I wasn't too happy. But I got myself composed and called my dad at home to tell him what happened. Dad drove out to pick us all up and the first thing he did was make sure everybody was okay. As we were driving home, he turned to me and said, "Well, it looks like you got into your first accident." He wasn't mad. He wasn't upset. And he didn't take my license away. He just saw it for what it was—an accident. He couldn't have been more understanding. Even to this day, I can't believe his reaction. He was more concerned above anything else. Dad has always been that way. He's an optimist by nature and has always taken life's uncertainties and disappointments in stride.

(Photo Courtesy of Kevin Stocker)

Kevin Stocker and his dad, Charles (circa 1993).

I was crushed the day I was told by the Phillies that they had traded me to Tampa Bay. To me the Phillies were family. They drafted me. They signed me. They brought me up to the majors. And I had made a lot of friends in Philadelphia. My dad was there for me that day. I spoke to him by phone that afternoon, gave him the news, and he was very upbeat. He said, "Well it looks like you have a new challenge ahead of you. This is a good thing." He made sure to point out all the things about the trade that were good. He told me there wasn't one thing about it that was a negative. And except for the friends I was leaving behind, I agreed with him. Of course, my mom was just the opposite. She grabbed the phone and said, "Couldn't you move any closer?"

◆ Kevin Stocker is a shortstop for the Tampa Bay Devil Rays.

Michael Milken

Philanthropist and Financier

MY FATHER WAS ORPHANED AT A VERY young age. His mother passed away during the birth of her next child and his father was killed in a traffic accident when he was around 10. Consequently, family was always very important to him.

When I was very young, I used to travel with him on the weekends and during the summer to visit the clients from his law and accounting practice. I used to have a half-hour or sometimes an hour in traffic to ask him hundreds of questions. I could ask him a question about anything and he seemingly always knew the answer. He was my own special tutor.

Later, as I did good work in helping with clients' books, my father allowed me to ask the person who ran the company questions. It was my first introduction to business and was a large part of my cherished childhood.

(Photo: courtesy of Michael Milken)

Michael Milken and his dad, Bernard (circa 1948).

I learned a lot about people and their personalities from my father. His commitment to individuals was unbelievable. He taught me that when you take responsibility for something, you do your best and go beyond what's expected. He was incredibly wise, and over time I viewed my father more as a Rabbi than just a dad. I think in some ways his clients viewed him that same way.

He would answer all types of questions for his clients—particularly as he became a trustee for their estates and became an advisor to the children. He took these responsibilities so seriously. I would often mention to my father that he seemed more concerned about their business than they did! But he convinced me how important it was to fulfill your obligations. He taught me that in order to do a good job in giving someone advice, you had to study so many different things. You had to understand not only their business, but you also had to understand history, peoples' personalities, sociology, and what was important to them. He taught my brother and sister and me what it meant to take responsibility for someone else's life or someone else's business.

People talk often about quality of time when it comes to parenting. But it isn't just quality of time. It's also quantity of time. Even though my father was very busy, I got to ride with him and go for walks hundreds and hundreds of times.

When I was diagnosed with cancer seven years ago, I looked for different alternative treatments. One of them was aromatherapy. I found that my immune system was activated by the smell of pine trees, redwoods, or sequoias. What these smells brought back were memories of when I was very young. I used to get up early in the morning when we went on family trips and walk with my father around Lake Arrowhead in the mountains of Southern California. The memories were so strong that just the smell brought back memories of those special days. It actually activated my own immune system and I believe helped contribute to putting my cancer in remission. Even though my father isn't around anymore, his memory is with me in my own recovery from cancer.

When I think of my father today, I can't help but recall what an eternal optimist he was. He contracted polio at a very young age and as a result, he had one leg shorter than the other. But he never complained and it never kept him from dancing or from playing football with my brother and me. He always saw the cup as half full—not half empty. His attitude toward life was that no matter what disabilities or hurdles you have to overcome, there's always a way to solve the problem. He taught me that commitment to others and your family is the true measure of accomplishment. "Work's important," he said. "But your family should come first." I was very lucky to have my father stress to me at a very young age how important family is.

◆ Michael Milken and his wife of 32 years, Lori, are the parents of three children. Well known as a financier and philanthropist, he considers his most important role to be as a father.

Earl G. Graves, Sr.

Publisher, *Black Enterprise*

MY FATHER ALWAYS WANTED
something better for his family.
He was a child of immigrants
from the Caribbean island of
Barbados. He was orphaned in
this country at 16 and was self-
supporting from that age on. He
took care of himself and a
younger brother with his hard
work and entrepreneurial
instincts.

(Photo courtesy of Earl G. Graves, Ltd.)

Earl G. Graves, Sr.

I grew up in the Bedford-
Stuyvesant section of Brooklyn in
a brownstone house that we
owned on Macon Street. My
parents had struggled to raise
enough money to buy it. Dad was
a disciplined man who believed in
keeping his nose to the grindstone and in the power of ownership. "Never
rent, always own," he often admonished me. He practiced what he
preached and rented out the upper levels of our brownstone to help with
the mortgage and supplement the family income.

Dad wasn't a warm person. It wasn't like he was a cuddly father where
I would sit on his knee when he came home from work in the evening. My
father was much stricter than the parents of any of my friends. I didn't
have much time to stop and hang out on the way home from school. He
had my time and the time of my three younger siblings—Sandra, Joan, and
Robert—very structured. He treated us all with a very firm hand.

But he was a dad who wanted to give us things. We always had meat
from O' Henry's Chop House on West Fourth Street. I used to meet him

in the garment center where he worked and then we'd drive to this butcher shop. When we got home, he always made it a point to show my mother what he picked out. He'd say, "Look at these chops. Look at these steaks." It gave him an enormous amount of pride that he could provide this for the family.

Dad graduated from Erasmus High School in 1928 which was one of the best high schools in the city. Graduating from there was like having a college degree. But after graduation, the only job he could find was with the Overland Garment Company. He began as a clerk pushing racks of clothing through the garment district, and over the course of his twenty years with the company rose to assistant distribution manager.

But like most West Indians, he usually worked at least one other job as well. His lucrative side job was selling women's clothes on consignment out of our home. He would bring home samples of the products Overland made and he would sell them wholesale to people in the neighborhood. My father only made about $65 a week on his regular job, so this side job provided an extra $15 a week in income. That was a lot of money in those days and that was money right into his pocket.

He was a natural salesman. He'd flatter people to death. But if it didn't look good, he'd say, "I don't think it's the right thing for you." I thought this was ingenious. I thought he'd lose a sale with his honesty. But his honesty helped gain people's confidence. He took the time to romance the client. If a winter coat was marked at $10 and a woman tried to get him down to $7, he would offer instead to sell her two coats at $9 each.

As a boy I watched and listened, and I think without realizing it, I absorbed a great deal of business sense—as well as my penchant for doing deals—from my father. When I was selling flowers as a student on the campus of Morgan State, I would apply these same rules in salesmanship. And the reason that I've had success throughout my life is because—like my father—I'm a good listener and I do what I tell people I'm going to do. My father wanted me to do business and he prepared me for it by setting values and showing me the right way to live life.

Growing up, telling the truth was not an option. There was only one thing to do, and that was to tell the truth. I had a bad report card once and it was the type of report card I knew I couldn't show my father. So I didn't. I signed his name and brought it back to school. I would have gotten away with it too, but somebody in the neighborhood told my father that his kid's report card had not been good and he had to punish him. My father came home after hearing this. I was washing dishes and he said to me, "Tell me about your report card."

I said, "What report card?"

"That's what I want to know," he said.

I remember getting a whack that night that I will never forget. But I also remember the lesson—don't lie. I grew up better for that experience.

The good old days really were the good old days. We weren't poor. We just didn't have much money. I learned salesmanship and hard work from my father, and I learned discipline too. It was hard to appreciate it at the time, but his high demands and expectations made me a striver and a doer. And while his stern, aloof manner prevented us from ever being close, it made me determined to be close to my own children, which, I'm proud to say, I am.

◆ Earl G. Graves, Sr. is the publisher of *Black Enterprise* magazine.

Mike Ditka

Studio Analyst, *The NFL Today* on CBS

MY FATHER WAS THE MOST IMPORTANT INFLUENCE IN MY LIFE. WHEN I WAS growing up in Aliquippa, Pennsylvania, he taught me a lesson that has stayed with me in everything I've ever done: "You get out of life what you put into it." My brothers and sister and I saw my dad live this lesson every day of his life. He worked for the railroad that serviced the steel mill in town and he never missed a day. He even worked on Saturdays. He used to say, "If you are willing to go out and put in a hard day's work, there will usually be good results."

Consequently, Dad raised us pretty sternly. And I think the main reason for that was to make sure that when we got older, we didn't go to work in the mill. He wanted us to have a better life than he did.

Dad's rules were simple ones: Respect people and people's property, be on time, and always be courteous. He also taught us to work hard in school and in sports. As a kid growing up I made a lot of mistakes. But every time I got out of line, I got put back in line by my father. If I got a whipping at school, I automatically got a whipping at home. There was no "We're going to sue the teacher" or "We're going to sue the school" in my family. Instead, I'd get two whippings for the price of one!

I played football, baseball, and basketball in high school and my dad saw just about every game. Initially, I didn't really think I could play football because I was so small. But Dad encouraged me to keep working at it. He knew that I wasn't born the most talented guy as far as athletics were concerned, but he also knew that hard work pays off. Besides my practices at school, I devoted weekends and summers to improving on my abilities. My hard work and his encouragement eventually paid off. I was offered a football scholarship and became the first person in my immediate family to go to college.

Dad laid down the law a lot, but I think that scholarship is what he was working for. There was no way he could have afforded to send me to college. But with his encouragement and guidance, I became a decent enough athlete to get a scholarship. This was very gratifying to Dad. He saw there was fruit born out of our hard work and effort. Dad didn't say a lot, but he was very proud of my accomplishment.

(Photo courtesy of the Chicago Bears)

Mike Ditka

The one thing I regret about my relationship with my father is that we didn't spend more time with each other. Because Dad worked so hard and I was always playing sports, we didn't do a whole lot together growing up. Dad would come home late from work and I went to bed very early. All the years I was in high school I was in bed by ten o'clock!

When he finally was able to spend more time with me, I was already very busy with my coaching. As he grew older, though, we used to just sit down and talk for hours. We'd speak about things that we never discussed when I was growing up. Dad began to see what is important in life. He wanted to be friends.

One of the biggest singular highs in my life was winning the Super Bowl and my dad was there for that. I'll never forget the look on his face when I saw him in the locker room. He was beaming. He was just so proud.

Dad lived his life in a very simple way. He worked, he provided for his family, and he made a lot of sacrifices. He dedicated his life to making sure that we had a better life. He was a teacher, a mentor, and a protector. That's the essence of what a good father is. And he fulfilled those roles magnificently.

◆ Mike Ditka is a studio analyst for "The NFL Today" on CBS. He is a member of the Football Hall of Fame and was head coach of the Chicago Bears team that won Super Bowl XX in 1986.

Carlos Gutierrez

President and CEO, Kellogg Company

I WAS BORN IN HAVANA, CUBA, WHERE MY FATHER OWNED HIS OWN BUSINESS. He grew pineapple and exported it to the U.S. Cuba was wonderful back then. We had a lovely house and Dad was a well-respected businessman in the community. The Castro revolution changed everything.

When I was seven years old, Dad left his business behind and moved us to Miami Beach. All we had was our bags and $2,000. At the time we thought Fidel Castro would only last a few months so we might as well go on a little holiday. After nine months though, we realized that Castro wasn't going away and that we were going to stay in this country. My father recognized our reality and he confronted it directly and honestly.

"We're not going back to Cuba," he told my mother, brother, and me.

This decision was very emotional for my father. He loved his country and he loved the life that he had. Now he had lost all of that. But the special thing about my dad was that even though it was so unbelievably disappointing and painful, he was still able to just deal with it, pick himself up, and try to create something new for himself and his family. He had the strength to not only deal with this loss, but to also make a new life in the United States.

My dad moved us around very often after leaving Cuba to find work and provide for his family. Even at a very young age, I began to appreciate all he was doing to make our lives better. There were times when I knew we were worse off than what I was accustomed to. Dad eventually got a job with a food company in Mexico. But my dad, deep down, wanted to get back to having his own business the way he had in Cuba. It was a dream he was never able to achieve.

My father went from being a very prominent and very well-off Cuban businessman to having virtually nothing. Through this experience, I learned that life can sometimes present you with some very difficult circumstances, and how you deal with them and the grace you show under fire will say a lot about your character. Because of what he went through, my dad instilled in me values of responsibility, hard work, and integrity.

Business in our household was what you were supposed to do. Cubans love business. It's a part of our culture. Consequently, I had no doubt or reservation that when I got older I would be in business just like my dad. The reason I liked business is because I liked the way he did it. He was even-handed with everybody. When I used to go to work with my father, I would literally just sit there and watch. He had a very forceful and charismatic personality. Everyone loved him.

In my junior and senior years in high school, while my friends were working at 7-11s and gas stations, I put on a coat and tie and sold magazine subscriptions. The experience that my father went

(Photo courtesy of Carlos Gutierrez)

Carlos Gutierrez with his dad, Pedro.

through encouraged me to do this. It was also something I was expected to do and something I wanted to do. From early on in life, I couldn't wait to get older so I could be in business.

The big business lesson I learned from my dad is that success is about results. Anything else is fluff. For him and for me the bottom line is what's important. He also taught me that your word is absolutely critical and that if you shake hands on something, you absolutely have to deliver.

I entered the food business in 1975 when I joined Kellogg's. The reason that I've enjoyed this company so much is because it has many of those same values that I learned at home. Kellogg's is very much into integrity, family values, and results. And the fact that my father was in the food business all of his life made the company even more attractive to me.

My father passed away in 1994 right before I was promoted to Kellogg's President of Asia/Pacific. He was so proud of my success and throughout my rise within the company, he was my closest advisor. Before he died, he told me the day would come when I would be President and CEO of Kellogg's. He had always supported me but this gave me a great deal of confidence. He was my mentor, my role model, and my hero. He was everything to me—and he still is. He would have been very proud if he could see me today.

◆ Carlos Gutierrez is the President and CEO of Kellogg Company. He and his wife, Edilia, live in Battle Creek, Michigan. They have three children.

Michael Chang

Professional Tennis Player

I GREW UP IN A CLOSE-KNIT FAMILY, so everything we did was very family-oriented. Whether we were playing in a tennis tournament or whether we were fishing on the weekends, everything involved the family. If my dad was out playing, we'd go out and watch him. If my brother Carl was playing, we'd go out and watch Carl.

(Photo courtesy of Octagon Athlete Representation)

Michael Chang with his dad, Joe, and older brother Carl.

In many ways, my dad made some very big sacrifices for us growing up. When we lived in San Diego, he still worked up in Orange County. Everyday he would get in his car and drive an hour and a half just to go to work. One of the reasons that he did that was so that Carl would be able to finish high school in San Diego. Dad realized how important that was to him and in order to make Carl's life better and less stressful, he simply made this sacrifice. A lot of that had to do with how much he loved us and just how much he wanted the best for us. Dad worked very hard but he was also incredibly dedicated to his children.

When Dad came home at the end of the day, he'd get a little something to eat and then he'd go out and play tennis with us for about an hour and a half. If we wanted to go out and play tennis at ten o'clock at night, my dad was more than willing to do it. Never once did he say, "No, I had a long day at work. I'm tired." He just grabbed his racket and drove us down to the neighborhood courts. We were just so blessed to have such a caring father.

I don't come from a very wealthy family, so Dad always stretched the family's money. Carl would take one tennis lesson one week and I would take a lesson another week. While we practiced, Dad sat on the sideline and took notes on what the teaching pro was trying to have us learn. The following week he took us out on the neighborhood tennis court and tried to incorporate those lessons into each of our games.

We never thought we'd make tennis our career. My dad just saw that we enjoyed ourselves and were getting better at it. He never thought twice about taking the time or spending the money to help us improve. My parents' philosophy was to let my brother and me try to find something that we really enjoyed. Once we found that, they would try to help us become the best at it. My dad used to say, "I don't care what you want to be as long as you strive to be the best at it." That was a great approach. As I found my talent in tennis, my dad always let me know that he supported me—and loved me.

That philosophy has also helped me so much in my career. When I walk off a court—whether I've won or I've lost—I always take comfort in the fact that my family is still there supporting me and loving me. Particularly in a sport like tennis, that is something that is very important. You are often judged by how you play. But my dad has always loved me for me. That unconditional support has always been a great comfort.

I come from a Christian family, so those values and morals are very important to me. I think that what some people don't realize is that when a child grows up, time goes by extremely fast. Time is not something that you can ever get back. The time that my dad spent with me has been very instrumental in my life. Not only did it keep our family very close, but it made it easier for him to understand me and for me to understand and respect him. I never realized the scope of the sacrifices that my dad made for us while we were growing up. I sort of took it for granted. However, now that I'm older, I'm amazed at all that he did.

◆ Michael Chang is the winner of the 1989 French Open and a two-time member of the U.S. Davis Cup team.

Jim Perdue

Chairman and CEO, Perdue Farms, Inc.

I GREW UP ON MY FAMILY'S FARM and chickens were always a part of our lives. We hatched baby chicks, fed them, and grew them, and in 1968, Dad bought an old plant in downtown Salisbury for processing them. It was the typical family business. My older sisters worked in the office along with my mom, who was the company payroll clerk. My dad, though, was the real workaholic. He commonly worked 18-hour days. He'd come home around six at night, eat dinner, and then he'd go back to work until two or three o'clock in the morning. And after getting four hours of sleep, he'd be up first thing in the morning.

(Photo courtesy of Perdue Farms, Inc.)

Jim Perdue and his dad, Frank (circa 1999).

What I learned most from my father was how strong his work ethic was. I would ride around with him to farms when he would sell baby chicks and I was always impressed with his sales ability. He was truly passionate with the farmers as to why they ought to buy from him.

His integrity was beyond reproach. If he made a promise about quality or delivery time, he kept it. To this day, when my dad tells a supermarket chain we will do something, everybody in this company knows that we will do it. My dad also started a tradition in this company—the open-door policy. If anybody had a problem, they could call Frank Perdue. That policy applied to customers, farmers, or an associate in the plant.

His attention to detail is amazing. In 1968, Dad decided to sell chickens with our name on them to butcher shops in New York. For six months, he walked from butcher shop to butcher shop and asked them what they wanted in a chicken. He then wrote down their answers on yellow legal pads. One day, he left one of those pads in a phone booth at the airport. When he went back to the phone booth, it was gone. Most people would be upset and move on. But not my dad. He called the airport authority to find out what landfills they take their garbage to, and then spent all day on this garbage pile until he found his pad. When he focuses on something, it consumes him! Those yellow pads are in our archives today and serve as the backbone of this company.

I always worked summers with my dad, so when I graduated from college it seemed only natural to join him in the family business. But after only nine months, I decided to leave. I wasn't enjoying it. In fact, I was miserable. And in retrospect, it was a good decision to make. It's very hard to work in a family company when your name is on the sign outside the door. When you get a pat on the back you're not sure if you are getting it because of who you are or because of the job you did. Confidence is something you learn, it is not something that you are born with. I felt it was important for me to get out and try to figure out who I was other than working in the company.

My dad always said, "You have to enjoy what you do in life, otherwise you will not be able to reach your full potential."

I moved to the West Coast and worked in the aqua-culture business for a full decade. Dad respected my decision. He could tell I wasn't happy. But he always wanted me to come back—of course, only if I wanted to and only if I enjoyed it. When I was 31, I had grown some confidence and matured. I wanted to come back and Dad couldn't have been happier. But he didn't put me to work in the executive office. Instead, I ended up working in a processing plant for four years.

Dad said, "If you don't understand the kind of work it takes to be successful at that level, then it is hard to make the right decisions when you are at this level."

That decision was right on target. Nepotism is a dangerous thing in a company unless the people respect you. And one of the keys to respect is knowing what they go through.

I have three children now and based on my own experience, I see how important it is to do what you really want to do. As a result, I tell my kids the same thing my dad told me, "You have to enjoy what you do in life. Otherwise you will not be able to reach your full potential."

The other thing I learned from my father is to have balance between work and family. I watched my father work 18 hours a day all throughout my childhood. He and my mother divorced in the late '60s and I'm sure it was because he spent too much time in the business.

I've realized that there's enough work for me to do 24 hours a day, 7 days a week. But if you don't have balance in your life, then you are not going to be as productive in your career. Consequently, I spend more time with my family than my father did with us. I learned so much from my father about this business, but he also taught me in some indirect ways about the importance of fatherhood.

◆ Jim Perdue is the chairman and CEO of Perdue Farms, Inc.

Bob Vila

Host, *Home Again*

MY DAD WAS BORN IN CUBA IN 1915, BUT HE HAD THAT OLD AMERICAN pioneer ethic. In the mid-1940s, he began building our modest family house in a quiet, middle-class section of Miami. In his free time he was always adding on to the house or improving it in some way. By 1956, he had already built a second house on the back end of the property. That ended up coming in handy because after the Castro revolution in 1959, we ended up having quite a few relatives living in the cottage.

Dad was a self-taught man. Without the help of a book or trade school, he learned by himself how to hustle concrete blocks, lay block, string a line, and mix concrete. He was extremely competent and I was his shadow on all of these projects.

I would ask, "Can I mix the concrete?"

"Sure," he'd say, "but you have to do it like this."

He was always very patient—but also instructive. He would never forbid me from trying anything. As a result, I learned a lot about construction and home repairs—which certainly has come in handy with the work I do today!

Dad also taught me a lot about straight shooting. I don't believe much in subterfuge and neither did he. My father was straightforward and honest, and that's where I got my own aversion to the sins of cheating, lying, and stealing.

During the 1950s, Dad was heavily involved in the fight against Castro and communism. He went back to Cuba for two years to gather information for U.S. intelligence on the revolutionary movement. For two years after we returned to the U.S. from Cuba, there was still a great deal of faith that it was only a matter of months before Castro would be toppled. But after the Bay of Pigs Invasion and the Cuban Missile Crisis, Dad pretty much decided that his life was here in America. I was only 13 when my father decided that this was his new homeland.

Dad dedicated himself to assimilating into America. He saw it as his duty to make the lives of his two children better than the life he had. In order to do this, he took on two jobs. He had a Cuban coffee business and a wholesale milk route. I still remember the smell of coffee permeating our house! After Mom and Dad put us to bed, they would go into this empty room in the house and grind and package the coffee beans.

He really devoted all of his energies to his family. Even in the '60s, going to the University of Florida—which I did—was a reach financially for somebody like my dad. But Dad never complained. He simply worked harder to pay for it. I learned from him that you just never lie down. Dad knew that he had a family to protect and take care of. He was just indefatigable and it's a work ethic that I've never questioned.

My father passed away in 1990, but by that time he had seen his grandchildren, seen my successes, and seen my television career get underway. There's very much a sense that all that my father achieved was achieved here. It made him a tremendous optimist to know that anything was possible in America.

◆ Bob Vila is America's best-known authority on home renovation and design. He has authored several books and CD-ROMs, and his nationally syndicated show, *Bob Vila's Home Again*, is celebrating its 10th anniversary season.

(Photo courtesy of Dera & Associates, Inc.)

Bob Vila and his family (with dad, Roberto, mom, Esperanza, and sister, Teresa).

Phil Mickelson

PGA Golfer

THE GREATEST COMPLIMENT I COULD EVER PAY MY DAD—AND THE ONE THING that I'm most appreciative about—is that he never pushed me in one direction. Instead, he gave me, as well as my brother and sister, every opportunity to succeed at whatever it was we chose.

When I was 11 years old, I had just won a tournament in junior golf and I was feeling pretty good about myself and my game.

"Dad, I want to play golf for a living," I announced. "I think I could be a pro."

"You know that would be great," he said. "If that's what you want, I'll try to give you every opportunity to play and practice. But I just want you to realize that very few people succeed at that out of the hundreds of people that try."

Dad stressed the importance of an education as something to fall back on. But he also helped me pursue my dream. He gave me every opportunity to play golf and to succeed at it. He's always been a great teacher and I learned so much from him. But when I was 12 and I had surpassed his knowledge of the game, he hooked me up with some local pros. I was able to work with them to try to get to the next level.

My dad is also probably the most patient individual I have ever met. He always explained why and how to do things—whether it was why I should try to make a certain change in my golf swing or how an automobile ran. He showed a tremendous amount of patience.

In seventh grade, my father was our coach when we got knocked out of the little league championship tournament. After the game, he got the team together.

"Listen, you guys accomplished a lot," he said. "Look at where your skill level was when you started and look at your skill level now. Be proud of the things that you've accomplished. Don't dwell on the fact that you've lost one game. Out of all the teams in the league, only one team was going to walk away winning their last game."

My dad had a way of making the team feel good—even after a very disappointing loss. He also had a way of instilling confidence in everybody. For the kids that were less skilled, he spent more time with them explaining the fundamentals of baseball so that they would improve. I still remember parents wanting their kids to be on my dad's team because he was the kind of manager that didn't really care if we won or lost. He cared about seeing the guys improve.

(Photo courtesy of Cornerstone Sports)

Phil Mickelson and his dad, Phil, Sr.

When I was 15, I played in my first American Junior Golf Association Tournament in Tucson. On the first day, I shot a 74, which turned out to be a good round. I was one or two shots off the lead. But the second day I went out, I shot an 88. I was very disappointed. We then had to drive back home to San Diego six and a half hours in a motor home. The whole way back we discussed the round, areas of my game where I could improve, some of the decisions that I made and why I made them. He never criticized me. Instead, he listened. And if he disagreed, he talked about it. Even at my most disappointing moments, he was really upbeat and positive.

In his own right, my father has accomplished so much that goes entirely unnoticed. Before his career as a commercial airline pilot, he was an incredible fighter pilot in the Navy. He was asked to teach at "Top Gun" and was even assigned to the Blue Angels. There are just so many things that he has done that make him a very interesting individual.

My dad is the one man that I look up to the most. There are a lot of great professional golfers that I respect and love to watch. But I don't respect them in the same way that I love and respect my dad. The reason is that he gave—and continues to give—every year of his life to his children in helping them succeed in whatever they want to do. As he watches us succeed, he never takes any of the credit. He's such a selfless person.

When I said I would have left the U.S. Open early to be there for my child's birth, I know my father would have done the same thing. There would have been no hesitation on his part. What really disappoints me is that there are some men who would consider missing their child's birth for the opportunity to win a golf tournament. As my father taught me, there's nothing more important in the world than your family.

◆ Phil Mickelson was a member of the victorious U.S. Ryder Cup team in 1999. He is the winner of 14 PGA tournaments and was a four-time first-team golf All-American at Arizona State University.

Chuck Jones

Cartoonist

(Photo courtesy of Chuck Jones Enterprises. ©Warner Bros.)

Chuck Jones

MY DAD WAS ALWAYS STARTING new businesses. He wanted to provide in the best possible way for his four children. Although most of these businesses didn't succeed, Dad never lost faith. "Take success in stride," he would say, "and failure with your chin up." Actually there was a positive side to Dad's failed businesses. For each new enterprise he would buy acres of the finest Hammermill bond stationery and hundreds of boxes of pencils bearing the company name. When the venture failed, he passed those supplies on to me.

This is how I was introduced to the wonderful world of drawing. When I was five, I was doodling on a sheet of paper when Dad noticed that I was using both sides. He told me, "Respect your talent. You never know when you are going to make a great drawing. Suppose Leonardo da Vinci had painted the 'Mona Lisa' on one side of a canvas and the 'Last Supper' on the other. How would he ever hang it?"

As I grew up and became more interested in drawing as a career, Dad was always right there encouraging me. He was never critical, but he also never over-praised my work. This made me value his judgment even more.

My father also taught me the importance of reading. He said, "What good does it do you to know how to draw if you don't know what to draw about? You can only learn that by reading." One of his rules around the house was, "No talking at the breakfast table." He said, "In the entire history of man, nothing intelligent has ever been said at the breakfast table." As a result, he made us bring a book to the breakfast table and we each read. I always respected that.

My father said the most dangerous thing about success was the possibility of becoming complacent. He told me repeatedly, "If you rest on your laurels, you're finished." That is why no matter what I accomplish, I always know there are blank sheets of paper waiting for me on my desk and easel the next day. This never-ending challenge is what drives me and keeps me from becoming lazy. My father taught me a lot. But the most important thing he passed on to me was an old Spanish proverb: "The road is better than the inn." He first told me this when I was seven and he explained to me that it simply means the road in life continues. And he was true to his word. My father never retired. He died in his seventies and was actually building a house—with his own hands—at the time.

I'm 87 now and the lessons my father passed on to me more than three-quarters of a century ago are what keep me going. In the last five years, I've painted dozens of watercolor sketches of Warner Bros. characters and I've even written two books. Two years ago I won the Smithsonian Institute Medal, and last year I was inducted into the Art Club Directors Hall of Fame. I'm extremely proud of these achievements and I see no reason to ever stop. I'm just simply enjoying myself. As Dad used to say, "Retirement is just another way of making a reservation at the nearest funeral home."

◆ Chuck Jones is the creator of such popular Looney Tunes characters as Porky Pig, Daffy Duck, the Roadrunner, and Wile E. Coyote, among a host of others. He has illustrated over 300 films for Warner Bros. and is the recipient of four Academy Awards.

Bernadine Healy

President, American Red Cross

I GREW UP IN LONG ISLAND CITY, New York, where Mom and Dad ran a little business making mixed essential oils and selling them to companies that used fragrances and perfumes. We lived in the apartment upstairs.

My dad was a tough Irish Catholic who had a very strict sense of right and wrong. We lived next to our church and I attended the church's parish school. But in matters of the intellect, he was amazingly liberal. Growing up, I was an egghead and read all the time. I especially loved to read books that pushed the envelope in terms of school. In eighth grade I read *Why I'm Not a Christian* by Bertrand Russell and books by Tolstoy and Dostoyevski. Back then, the church banned books like those. But my father supported me 100 percent. He said, "You read any book you want. Books should challenge you."

(Photo courtesy of Dr. Bernadine Healy)

Bernadine Healy (front row, far left) with her family—father, Michael Healy, mother, Violet Healy (maiden name–McGrath), sisters, Michele Ubelaker, Suellen Manning, Catherine Kassens.

When it was time for me to go to high school, I was offered full scholarships to two very prominent parochial schools. I was also admitted to Hunter High School—a highly selective public high school for girls. The nuns and the priests in our church felt strongly that I should go to the parish schools. But Dad felt I would get a better education—a broader education—by going to Hunter. On the surface, Dad was very old-fashioned. But beneath that, he was quite progressive. Considering his background, he was amazingly open-minded.

He taught me early on that there were no limits to what I could accomplish as a woman. This was before women's lib was even a notion or concept! In those days, women couldn't go to Princeton or Yale and that outraged him. He felt that women were equal to men and that there should be no discrimination whatsoever. Even though there were very few women going into medicine in those days, when I told him I wanted to become a doctor, he was so supportive. He said, "You're my girl. You'd be better than any man in medicine!"

My father believed in education. When he was 12, he had to quit school to go to work. One continuing concern for my father was that he never completed his education. Consequently, his absolute priority was that his children would be educated and there would be no limits to their educational aspirations.

He used to tell us, "You want to go to Harvard. You go to Harvard. You just work hard and get a scholarship."

He believed that if you worked hard and you used your God-given talent, you could succeed. He was the eternal optimist and had unbelievable faith in this country. He worked hard to realize the American dream—especially for his children.

He was as proud when I graduated from grammar school with good grades as the day I received my medical degree from Harvard. My father saw every educational achievement or milestone as a major event for celebration. He valued that above all else.

After my sisters and I were educated—all on scholarships—Mom and Dad decided to go back to school. They each had to pass the high school equivalency exam just to gain entry to LaGuardia Community College. Dad was already in his sixties! After work every day, they'd ride the subway and go to class. They studied very hard and each of them got fabulous grades. Mother was 4.0 and Daddy was 3.9. When graduation day arrived, I was so excited and proud to see them in their caps and gowns. It was a wonderful day.

Mom and Dad didn't stop with an associate's degree. They each decided to go on to Baruch College in New York City to complete their bachelor's degree. But Dad got sick with cancer. I will never forget standing in the hospital room after he was told about the cancer.

He turned to me and said, "Bern, this means I won't be able to finish college."

That's my dad. He had that passion for education and the potential it created for you as a person. It wasn't just because you could get a better job. It was because of what it did for you inside—the way it expanded your thinking and your horizons. He saw education as one of life's greatest joys.

A lot of people stand for a lot of things. But my father lived what he stood for. That's what made him so special. He was a magnificent man who loved his family and believed in values of integrity, goodness, and kindness. It's almost twenty years since he died and I don't think a day goes by that Dad isn't with me.

I think that the fact that my father had so much confidence in me helped me develop my potential. He never let me get discouraged. He gave me security and let me know that he would be there for me "come hell or high water." I think that was the greatest gift Dad gave me; a gift I hope will endure with my children.

If my father were alive when I was appointed to head the American Red Cross, he'd say, "That's my girl!"

◆ Dr. Bernadine Healy is the president of the American Red Cross. She formerly served as the dean of the medical school at Ohio State University and prior to that was the director of the National Institutes of Health.

Jan-Michael Gambill

Professional Tennis Player

I STARTED PLAYING TENNIS WHEN I WAS FIVE YEARS OLD AND BASICALLY TOOK up the sport because I wanted to be around my dad. Dad would take me to the local tennis club and keep an eye on me there because there was nobody to take care of me at home. Even as a young boy, I would love to watch my dad play. And after awhile, I wanted to get out on the court and play with him.

Growing up, my dad was an avid tennis fan and we would watch matches together. My heroes—McEnroe, Connors, Agassi, and Becker—were his heroes. So tennis was a bond we had from very early on. I played my first tournament when I was nine, and I think from then on, it was in my heart and I really wanted to play professionally.

My dad has been with me from the start. He was my first coach and he remains my coach. Besides teaching me the skills I need on the court, he has instilled in me a tremendous drive and focused intensity.

He has always stressed upon me the need to treat other people well. It goes back to the "Golden Rule"—treat people like you wanted to be treated yourself. I learned so much from him by example and watching him.

When I was nine, I entered my first tennis tournament in Spokane. It was a local tournament for 10-year-olds, and needless to say, my dad was there to watch me. This was a big deal to me. It has always meant so much to me to know that I have my father behind me. I played very well that weekend and eventually got to the finals. But I met my match in a much bigger 10-year-old and lost. I was very disappointed. After the match, I cried. I felt like I let myself down and I let my dad down.

My father came down from the stands after the final point and saw how upset I was. He put his arm around me, told me how proud he was of me, and then said, "This match is not the end of the world. It's the beginning of a bright future. There will be plenty of tournaments to play in and this loss is not that big a deal." We then sat down in the stands that surrounded the court and talked about the match—what I did right and what I did wrong. He basically told me to use this loss as a learning experience. The next year, when I was 10, I played in this same local tournament and won. It was a great feeling and I think that on some level my father may have been happier than I was!

When I lose, my dad has taught me to use it as a learning experience. Even when I win, Dad taught me that I can learn a lot from what I did wrong. The main thing I learned from him is to be upbeat and positive because I'll always get another chance.

My goal over the next few years is to be among the top 10 players in the world. I know this will require a lot of hard work and effort. But I consider myself lucky that I have such a great father to help me achieve my dream. Tennis is often called an individual sport, but my father is a partner in my reaching this goal.

◆ Jan-Michael Gambill is among the top 10 tennis players in the United States and is considered one of the rising stars on the ATP Tour.

(Photo courtesy of Jan-Michael Gambill)

Jan-Michael Gambill and his dad, Chuck.

James P. Hoffa

President, International Brotherhood of Teamsters

I WAS RAISED BY A FATHER WHO WAS EXTREMELY SELF-CONFIDENT AND FEARLESS. He never ran from his problems or his disappointments. Rather, he confronted all of his challenges directly. In fact, he was quite open about these things and never shielded the family from them. We would sit down and honestly talk about them around the dinner table. Even as a young boy, he shared with me the very real problems that confronted our family.

My father taught me that it's important to have the traits of self-confidence and self-sufficiency to be successful in life. I attribute my successes and my ability to project my self-confidence to my supporters to my father and the way I was raised.

Every year since 1949, we would go hunting and fishing together at this remote cabin on a lake in Western Upper Michigan.

We would spend a tremendous amount of time together there. Part of the purpose of these trips was that my dad wanted to teach me to be self-sufficient.

He would leave me in the woods all by myself for hours. He would tell me what to do if I got frightened or hungry or cold. The idea was to instill me with confidence. I became so confident that whenever we would go hunting, this was an aspect of the trip that I looked forward to. It made me strong and also proved the trust that I had in him.

My father also stressed the importance of an education. My father was brilliant, but he only went to the eleventh grade. Despite this lack of education, he was able to rise above all of that to become one of the most powerful labor leaders in America.

But he realized that his situation was rare. He always said, "If you don't have an education, you'll never make it." He assured us that this was the best way to ensure a happy and fulfilling life. There was never a question about whether my sister and I would go to college. In fact, each of us also went on to law school and my sister is now a judge in St. Louis. I think the success that each of us has had can be attributed to the direction my father provided us at such an early age.

Dad often took me to work with him, so we had a lot of quality time together. As a young boy, I would see how much my father loved the rank and file members of the Teamsters and how much they loved him. Fifty or sixty people would line up to see him on a Saturday at Local 299 in Detroit. Afterwards, we would go to a membership meeting and people would just line up to shake his hand. It would take hours for him to get out of the meeting hall because people wanted to share the moment or share their problems with him.

They loved him because he had this tremendous personality and charisma and a genuine love for the membership. He treated everyone with dignity and kindness and always with a smile. He was so sincere. To this day,

(Photo courtesy of the International Brotherhood of Teamsters)

James P. Hoffa with his dad, James R. Hoffa (circa 1962).

people come up to me and talk about him like they just met him. I still carry this with me.

I was seven years old the first time I went with my dad to Local 299. On the way home, he always said the same thing—"The Teamsters members are the most important people in the world." That's the way I was raised and that's what he taught me.

My father disappeared in 1975 when I was 34. But if my father were alive today, I think he would be so happy and so proud of what we have been able to accomplish and with what we plan to do with the Teamsters Union— making it strong and making it a union everybody can be proud of.

◆ James P. Hoffa is the president of the International Brotherhood of Teamsters, the same union that his father, James R. Hoffa, headed from 1957–1967.

Kathleen Kennedy Townsend

Lieutenant Governor of Maryland

I REMEMBER LOTS OF THINGS ABOUT MY FATHER, BUT MY GREATEST MEMORY was how much he liked to play with us—his children. When he came home from work he liked to have "tickle-tumbles," which would mean he'd grab you and tickle you and roll around on the bed. There was a lot of physical contact with Dad and he was always so warm and cuddly.

If it was Saturday morning, that meant one thing to my dad and my brothers and sisters—football. It would be a rare Saturday when we didn't play! We were an active family and Dad kept us busy. He loved to take us riding, skiing, hiking, or sailing. He just loved to spend his free time with all of us.

My father was also very keen on having us understand politics and public service. When other children were three years old and they'd go to the playground, my mother was taking me to the Senate Racket Committee Hearing when he was the chief counsel. As we got older, we would discuss important issues and we would be quizzed on current events or on history. He wanted us to understand this country and this would often mean road trips to visit Civil War battlefields in Virginia or in Maryland.

At night, not only were we quizzed at the dinner table, but after our homework, there would be nightly prayers. We'd say the rosary together and my father would read a chapter from the Bible.

Dad would often quote St. Luke's admonition: "From those who have been given much, much will be expected." When my father came back from a trip to Mississippi, he came into our beautiful dining room with crystal on the table and freshly pressed linen tablecloth and told all of my brothers and sisters how he had seen children with distended stomachs and families of 12 living in small shacks. I can still remember vividly when he told us, "I've just come back from Mississippi. Do you know how lucky you are? Do something for your country."

We learned from my father by example. At Christmas time, he would often have parties at the Justice Department and later in his Senate office for kids who often didn't have the ability to celebrate Christmas so well. I remember a number of times we'd go to New York and rather than go directly to midtown Manhattan, which was where we'd stay, he would drive us through Harlem so that we would see another side of life. We understood that we were very fortunate.

The lessons I learned from my father were not only taught by example, they were also taught explicitly. We were taught to be honest, not to tattle tale, to defend your brothers and sisters, and to always try your hardest.

I remember once my brother and I were sailing in a race and we tipped over. I thought it was kind of funny. But of course it also meant that we didn't win the race. When we told our father what had happened, we thought he'd think it was funny too. But he

(Photo Credit: The John F. Kennedy Presidential Library. Courtesy of Kathleen Kennedy Townsend.)

Kathleen Kennedy Townsend with her dad, Robert F. Kennedy.

was hardly amused. He said, "You shouldn't have tipped over. You were supposed to sail to win." He was pretty tough. But behind this stoicism, was the sense that our father wanted us to take ourselves seriously. Don't futz away your time. Even when we had fun—skiing, hiking, riding, or playing football—we were supposed to take those things seriously.

After his brother died, Dad would always read the Bible. But he read many of the Greek tragedies as well. I think this helped him understand that much of life is about fate. He became very thoughtful about how to deal with tragedy. You go on and you don't shy away from what happened, but you don't complain.

When John Kennedy died, my dad wrote all of us a letter, and he ended it with the admonition: "As the oldest of the Kennedy grandchildren you have a particular responsibility now . . . be kind to others and work for your country." I think he understood that you always had to be kind. People suffer. And it's sad. And he taught us that we should always have empathy for those who suffer.

I certainly want my children to appreciate the fortune that has blessed them. And I hope that I've passed on from my father a sense that they should care about public life and get involved in public service.

◆ Kathleen Kennedy Townsend is the lieutenant governor of Maryland. She is the eldest child of the late Senator Robert F. Kennedy.

Michael Powell

Commissioner, FCC

CONTRARY TO WHAT MANY PEOPLE may assume, I did not grow up in some sort of military-disciplined household. Rather, it was a place of a lot of free form and a lot of fun. In the early years, my mother was a very central figure because Dad was off fighting in two wars and one hardship tour. So there were a lot of early absences. But as I became a pre-teen, he really became a featured part of my life and my primary role model. His motto was really simple and one that I loved: "I'm gonna teach you right and I'm gonna teach you wrong, and I'm gonna teach you to take responsibility for which path you choose. The rest is up to you." He didn't hammer me on every little thing I did—even on report cards. Sometimes he didn't even look at my grades! Instead he tried to invest in me the spirit that I should care more than anybody about how I'm doing in school or in life.

(Photo courtesy of Michael Powell)

Michael Powell with his dad, General Colin L. Powell (ret.).

My father's notoriety came rather late in my life. He didn't become a one-star general until I was in high school. So growing up, we were the average army family. We just figured he'd retire at colonel like everyone else!

189

When we would move from army base to army base, he always tried to make it the most exciting thing on the face of the earth. In my last year of high school we moved to Colorado, and like our previous moves, Dad made it a huge production. He sent away for lots of pamphlets and brochures on how wonderful everything was around Colorado Springs. He even found all of our friends for us in advance. He actually knocked on doors in the neighborhood where we were going to live and found every child of a similar age for me and my younger sisters! He then put together a full report on what the lay of the land was like—where our school was, where the best pizza place was, and what there was to do for entertainment.

Once that was taken care of, we didn't move directly to our new home. Instead, Dad took time off, piled us in the back of the station wagon and we drove to every cheesy American landmark you could possibly go to between Northern Virginia and Colorado Springs—everything from Mount Rushmore to the corn palace in upper North Dakota to the Harley Davidson motorcycle convention in Sturgis, South Dakota. It was fun for us, but we actually had the most fun watching him get so obsessed with trying to make our move as stress-free as possible. I think that's what makes him such a great dad. When you have a father whose career could result in him never coming home again, it creates an interesting environment. In hindsight, my parents were incredible at making our home warm and safe and nestlike.

Our household was driven by the same values that my dad learned from his Jamaican father. Sometimes you'd swear he was "Poppy." He always taught us about self-responsibility. He'd lecture us by saying, "No matter what you think went wrong, before you even say a word or point a finger, you'd better go through your own performance and determine what you could have done better."

A perfect example of that is in dealing with issues like race. There can be a tendency if you're so inclined to quickly jump to some conclusion that you were discriminated against or someone didn't like you because of who you are. But that was intolerable in our household. We were taught to go look in the mirror. He'd say, "Maybe it's not fair that you have to be two or three notches better to get the same credit as someone three notches below, but that's too bad. Get over it and get there." He told us time and time again, "You've got to live to make discrimination somebody else's problem, not yours." We had to take care of ourselves and our own performance first and foremost.

Patriotism was also an important value Dad instilled in me. But not in some corny, military way someone might assume. He'd tell us that we were blessed to be in a place of extraordinary opportunity. We were taught to really love where we are and to be strong supporters of the country—its purpose, its past, its destination. For Dad, that was especially meaningful. His parents left the Caribbean for New York to give him and his sister a chance. To see those opportunities come through in spades instilled this wonderful sense of optimism and possibility in our household.

Of course, it wasn't always a bed of roses growing up and Dad had a subtle way of letting us know when he didn't approve of our actions. I rarely drank beer in high school, but I remember one time when I stayed out late and probably drank too much. I had a very bad morning and it was turning into a very bad afternoon. I was feeling miserable. It was one of those Virginia days of 95-degree heat and 95-percent humidity. At about three in the afternoon, Dad came into my room and said, "I think you need to cut the grass." All I could think of was how this chore was going to hurt a lot. The smell of gasoline coupled with the heat was not going to do much for my hangover!

"Dad," I said, "I can cut it tomorrow."

He replied immediately, "No, I think you should cut it now."

I pleaded, "I'm really tired." I was hoping that might tug at his heart strings a little bit.

But the sympathy routine clearly wasn't working. He looked me over in my bed and said, "Well if you weren't out so late, maybe you wouldn't be so tired."

This was Dad's way of letting me know I wasn't fooling anybody. He didn't confront me about my hangover. Instead, he made me suffer! He clearly made his point and I never did that again.

My greatest fear growing up was disappointing my dad. I don't ever remember being hit by him. From time to time, though, I received a yelling—which could be extremely scary coming from a senior infantryman!

I served in the ROTC and my dad commissioned me at William & Mary. My favorite picture on earth is of him and me standing with our arms around one another—me in my brand new butter bars and uniform and him in his uniform—he was a two-star general then. That is an amazing bond with a father. I loved being a soldier with him. There was something so cool about wearing the same uniform, serving the same cause, and sharing thoughts about all of that together. Nothing's cooler than saluting your father. If he was in uniform and I was in uniform, we'd do two things. We would salute and then we would kiss and hug.

A lot of people say to me, "Your father is so great." And I always have the same response, "Well, for what it's worth, he's everything you think he is."

◆ Michael K. Powell, the eldest child of General Colin L. Powell (ret.), is a commissioner on the Federal Communications Commission.

Leon Botstein

President, Bard College

MY FATHER TAUGHT ME WHAT IS REALLY VALUABLE IN LIFE. TO HIM, PERSIAN rugs, jewelry, and furs were all nonsense. He understood from World War II that material things are of no real importance. Money was a necessity and one can't fly in the face of it, but he had no need for luxuries. He didn't miss having a Saks Fifth Avenue suit or eating in Lutece—it never would have occurred to him. He was happiest with the simplest of things. He thought Kentucky fried chicken at a diner was just the end-all and be-all of cuisine!

When it came to education, though, money was important. If somebody had told him tuition at college was fifteen times as much, he wouldn't have blinked an eye. He would never have said, "Don't go to that college. It's too expensive." He insisted. He would have mortgaged everything. He would have lived in a hut to pay for anything that had to do with education. In fact, he paid to educate extended members of the family.

My father loved his work—he was a radiation oncologist and a professor of medicine. He didn't work to earn money. He worked to gain meaning in life. He worked in order to think of himself as having made a contribution to the world he lived in. His attitude was, "I don't think I have a right to exist except in so far as it can be measured by what I do for other people."

He was actually amazed that somebody paid him to do what he loved. He loved teaching. He loved the research. He loved fighting on the frontiers of medicine. He loved the excitement and the ingenuity of the new residents at the hospital. Many times he was offered jobs in private practice on Park Avenue. These jobs would have paid four times as much, but he had the same response to every job offer. He said, "What, are you crazy? For what?" I have very much the same attitude. If someone offered to pay me $500,000 to take on a new career, I wouldn't do it. I'm amazed that somebody pays me to teach. Someone pays me to run a college. Someone pays me to give concerts. I learned from my father that love of work is what life is all about.

I also learned a very important lesson about loss from my father. He was terribly candid and looked life straight in the eye with all of its difficulties. When I was 34, I had a daughter who was hit by a car while waiting for a school bus. Abby was not quite eight years old when she passed away. It was devastating. The loss of a child is one of the most painful things a parent can experience. My parents were also very attached to the grandchildren and I knew I had to tell them what happened. I drove to the hospital where both my parents worked and broke the terrible news. This was the only time that I saw my father cry.

My mother and father stayed with me through the funeral and for several weeks they paid daily visits to the house. He was terribly distraught by Abby's death, as was I. But he talked me through my pain. It was very typical of my father. He said, "You are extremely lucky. You had this wonderful daughter for eight wonderful years. You should be grateful for that. You have another wonderful daughter—Sarah. Be grateful for her. She's a terrific girl. Yes it's painful. But you must look on and be grateful for what was."

My father taught me not to look at Abby's death purely as a complete loss, but as a gift for which I should be grateful and not feel sorry for myself. My father was crucial in my ability to pull myself together as an adult. He was indispensable to me. I don't think I would have been able to go on without his help.

◆ Leon Botstein is the president of Bard College in Annandale-on-Hudson, New York.

(Photo courtesy of Bard College)

Leon Botstein

Kobe Bryant

Guard, Los Angeles Lakers

MY FATHER HAS ALWAYS BEEN A down-to-earth kind of guy. That was something that always stood out in my mind growing up. He never put himself on a pedestal.

When I was about five years old, we moved to Italy from Philadelphia so that Dad could play in the European Basketball League. He had been a fairly anonymous player in the NBA. But in Italy, he was "the man." Despite this celebrity status, he always treated people with respect and treated them the way he wanted to be treated. That was a very special lesson that I learned just by watching him.

Growing up in Italy, he taught me that family comes before anything. Family values were always at the top of what he considered important. The whole family—Mom and Dad, my two older sisters, and I—would just be together. We would watch a movie together, we would wrestle each other, we would go to the playground together. We have always enjoyed each other's company.

My father never gave me just one path to go down in life. It was always my decision. Playing basketball for a living wasn't a conscious

Kobe Bryant with his dad, Joe.

(copyright 2000 Andrew D. Berstein/NBA Photos) Photo Courtesy of SFX Sports.

decision. It just evolved, because I loved to play so much and I wanted to do it all the time.

In high school, when I considered turning pro, my dad was there for me, providing moral support. Although he played in the NBA and was somewhat familiar with what my life would be like, he helped me make my decision based on what was best for me. He encouraged me to do whatever my heart told me to do.

Dad never warned me of the risks involved in pro-basketball. He had complete faith in my abilities and what I could do. He used to tell me, "You can do anything that you put your mind to. There are no limits." This instilled in me a tremendous amount of confidence.

The foundation provided by my father also helped prepare me for the rigors of the NBA. That stable center is especially important here in Los Angeles where I have people tugging on me from all directions.

When I moved out to L.A., I was only 17. I knew that I wasn't ready yet for life on my own. So my family did something really amazing. Dad moved everyone—the whole family—into my house.

Just because I was going to the NBA didn't mean I had to walk away from my family before I was actually ready to do so.

The thing that is so special about my dad is that he has always had complete faith in me. He believed that I could evaluate every path that my life might go down and choose the one that was best for me.

After I made the announcement in my high school gymnasium that I was going to turn pro, I got home and he gave me a big hug.

"Kobe, I am happy for you and I am proud of you," he said. "Now let's go kick some butt!"

That really lightened things up and we started laughing.

It also symbolized everything about our relationship. There was a wide range of emotions for us that day in Ardmore. He was happy about my decision and about my future. But he was also a little sad because we were going to leave home.

By just supporting me in everything I do, Dad has made my transition to the pros rather smooth. He's a great father and a great friend. I couldn't have asked for a better dad.

◆ Kobe Bryant is an all-star guard for the Los Angeles Lakers.

Brian Roberts

President and CEO, Comcast

(Photo courtesy of Comcast Corp.)

Brian Roberts with his dad, Ralph.

I WAS 10 YEARS OLD WHEN I DECIDED I wanted to work for my dad's company. After selling his men's accessories business, my father had gotten into the cable business, and I was fascinated by it. I would go to his office on weekends and do odd jobs, punching payment coupon books and the like. During summer breaks in high school and college, he gave me more responsibility. I installed cable in people's homes. I climbed utility poles to string cable wires. I even sold cable door to door!

In the spring semester of my senior year in college, I had a talk with my dad. I told him that although I had received some very nice offers from some investment banking firms on Wall Street, what I really wanted to do was to work for Comcast—and for him.

He said, "Well that's very nice. But if you go to work for a Wall Street firm for a couple of years, you can learn how they think and bring that experience back here."

I told him, "I don't really want to work somewhere else. It just doesn't feel right."

Deep down I was worried that the time would never come for us to work together. He was already in his sixties, and I didn't want to spend a number of productive years working somewhere else. I thought, "What if something happened to him? We'd never have had the chance to work together." So I resisted.

At one point in our discussion, I said, "You're rejecting me. You must not love me."

This got to him. He finally gave in. But he quickly rid me of my fantasy of coming to our headquarters every day and working in our adjoining executive offices. He put me on the road.

First stop, our then brand new cable system in Trenton, New Jersey. Then on to Flint, Michigan, and several other stops. Dad wanted me to learn the business from every angle. He would tell me, "I'm not an expert in this business. I got into it late in life. But you're young. Go do it all and you'll learn this business from the ground floor."

This is what made my father such a good dad. He saw that I wanted to take on an important challenge. He instilled a lot of confidence in me. But he saw that I was aggressive and impetuous, and that I needed some latitude to develop my individuality. He didn't just allow that to happen, he encouraged it. He said, "Go take chances. Make mistakes. You'll learn so much."

Now I've worked for my father for almost 20 years, and in that whole time, he would tell you, I've never had a bad idea. Of course, he might react to something I say like this: "That's very interesting. Have you thought about doing it this way?" Implicitly, of course, he'd be saying my idea wasn't so hot, and I should look for another answer. But he never discouraged me.

There's a constructive way to give criticism and there's a destructive way. My father is clearly from the constructive school. In the formative years, a parent has to nurture a child and Dad always had this sixth sense to encourage, support, and share with me. He helped me grow in the company and grow as a person. He has been a true mentor and a great dad.

In both business and in family, Ralph instilled in me the idea of the Golden Rule—don't think just because you have an important position, that makes you a better person than the fellow who's filling your gas tank. There's a certain way to conduct yourself in all aspects of your life, with respect for others. My father has conducted himself in an exemplary fashion for the 40 years that we've been together.

On the business side, my dad has always set a tone of high integrity. When we say we're going to do something, we mean it. He started this company by investing the first $50,000. Together we built this company with billions of dollars in borrowed money. We have never missed an interest payment in 30 years. From that, we've built a company with a market value of over $50 billion, we employ over 20,000 people, and we have over 8 million cable subscribers. We also own QVC, Comcast SportsNet, and E! Entertainment, among other properties. And every step of the way, we've done this with respect for each other and for the people with whom we deal.

Maybe the most important thing I learned from my dad is how to balance family and business. This is not always easy. My memory as a boy is that he was home every night. When he walked in the door, his mind was on his wife and his five kids—not the office.

It's the ultimate dream to work with my father. I feel like I'm the luckiest person in the world because we're building this company together. Success is wonderful, but sharing it with someone is really what it's all about.

◆ Brian Roberts is the president and CEO of Comcast, the nation's fourth-largest cable company. His father Ralph started the business in 1963 with $5/month service in Mississippi.

Vince McMahon

Chairman, World Wrestling Federation

MY PARENTS WERE DIVORCED SHORTLY AFTER I WAS BORN AND I GREW UP ALL over North Carolina. My mom was married a lot of times and I didn't actually meet my dad until I was 12 years old. In fact, I didn't even know that my last name was McMahon for quite a number of years!

When we finally met, it didn't take any time at all for our relationship to become close. I fell in love with him the moment I saw him. It was a feeling I never had before. I didn't know that I had missed a dad—much less my father—until I met him.

During the holidays and every summer, I'd go and visit with my dad in Washington, D.C. He was already involved with what was then the Capitol Wrestling Corporation—which his father started—and controlled much of the early televised wrestling in the Northeast. It was so cool to hang around my dad with all of these giants and charismatic characters. I knew right away that wrestling was what I wanted to do with my life.

I was 27 when I joined my father's business full time. I had wanted to be in the business for many years, but my father wouldn't let me. He felt it was too speculative and wanted me to do something more secure. But that's not what I wanted. I wanted so badly to be in this business. After I pleaded with him for some time, he finally allowed me an opportunity to promote a wrestling match in Bangor, Maine. This was the furthest outpost of my dad's territory. He said he was having problems with a promoter up there who was stealing money.

"Look, you've been badgering me for so long," he said. "Don't ask me ever again to be in the business if you don't make this a success." And of course it was.

My performance career came later. One of my father's announcers quit on him right before a wrestling match in Pennsylvania. He wanted a huge increase in his compensation. Immediately before the show was to begin, he said, "Pay me that or I'm walking."

My dad felt his ultimatum was extremely unfair and told him to take a walk. I was so proud of my dad because he refused to be pushed. But he then turned to me 90 seconds later and said, "Congratulations. You now have another job. You're a television announcer!"

Vince McMahon

Of course, I had never done that before. And you could tell! I stumbled, fumbled, and bumbled. But my father supported me. The same night he gave me the announcer job, he said, "This isn't a temporary position. You've got this job permanently. So go do the best you can." He had enormous confidence in my abilities.

Once I was in business with my dad, I relished every second that I had with him. On occasion, people would ride in the car with us when we would travel from town to town. I'd actually get angry at that because I just wanted to spend time alone with my dad. It was a privilege to simply be around him.

Dad would impart little tidbits of wisdom about life when he was with me. I watched the way he conducted himself and I learned a lot from him. Even though I'm 53 now, there's not a week that goes by that I don't quote my dad. I don't even know if he knew he was teaching me. But he was.

My father had a strong sense of fairness—particularly to his employees. He always kept his word and his reputation in this business was impeccable. But what made him so special was his kindness toward others.

The last time I ever saw my dad was a long time ago. I was 38 at the time and it was just before he died. He had cancer and he was in the hospital. The old Irish value system is that you don't physically display affection for people and you don't necessarily say the words, "I love you." I was always different from my dad in that respect.

As I kissed him good-bye on his forehead, I fully expected to see him again. But he knew differently. Before I got completely out of the room, he yelled at me that he loved me. That is a moment I will never forget.

We both learned one thing in our relationship and it's rather tragic—we missed so much from each other by not being together as I was growing up. And that's something that I vowed would never happen with my family. I didn't want my children to miss out on what I had missed out on. My experience taught me that there's a certain responsibility that you have to have as a father.

I'm also different from my dad when it comes to affection. I must tell my kids several times a day that I love them. I also rarely miss a chance to hug and kiss them. I think that it's so important for children to know that they are loved.

Despite these shortcomings, my father was such a wonderful man. I think he'd be very pleased if he could see the WWF now. He's been dead almost 16 years, but I still miss my dad. I really do.

◆ Vince McMahon is the chairman of the World Wrestling Federation.

Dale Jarrett

1999 NASCAR Winston Cup Series Champion

WHEN I WAS BORN IN 1956, MY FATHER WAS RACING IN WHAT IS NOW THE Busch Grand National Division. He kept quite a schedule. Some weeks he raced five times. Other weeks it was just three. But despite his travel, my brother Glenn, sister Patty, and I never felt neglected.

As a young boy, I would travel with my dad in the summer to most of his races. Whether it was a race in Darlington or a race in Taladega, I was right there by his side. During that time, I paid close attention to him because I realized he was very successful in how he went about things. The biggest lesson I picked up was how well he treated people. It didn't matter if they were the sponsors of the car who came into the pit, the crewmen, or the fans, he seemed to treat everyone the same. He had a fondness for everyone and he always had the time for them. Sometimes, of course, he was extremely busy. But he always found the time for the fans and for the people who were there to support him.

My father has always been my hero. In fact, now that I'm older, my respect, admiration, and love for him have grown even more. I always looked up to him because he was not only a champion at what he did, but he somehow always found the time for his family. I see now how difficult that is and how difficult it must have been then with the schedule he had to keep. With as many races as he was running, I'm even more impressed! He always had time to answer my questions and get to as many little league games as he possibly could. Whatever it took, he tried to make it work.

My dad also stressed to our family that even though he couldn't always be there on Sundays, the rest of us had to be in church. Just because we were at a race in Charlotte, it didn't mean that I could skip my prayers. A lot of people look at me a little funny whenever I say I grew up in a Christian home that spent so many days on the road. But that's what we really did. Faith has always been an important element in our family.

My dad never pushed me into race driving at all. As a matter of fact, if anything, he steered me away a little—not because it's a bad sport, but because he knew how difficult a sport it is and how difficult it was to get to the top. I think that as a parent, you just always want the best for your kid. You don't want to see them struggle. You would like for everything to go smoothly. But once I did make that choice, he's been behind me 100 percent and been very helpful to me throughout my career.

Initially, though, Dad wasn't financially able to help me a lot. It's so different from getting involved in other sports. Racing takes money to get involved—not just talent. I think that actually worked to my benefit. It got me involved in every aspect of this business.

Dad taught me to go out and basically sell myself—a young man wanting to learn to race. We started a company and I basically ran it. I had to go out and obtain the sponsors on my own, hire a crew on my own, and also pay the bills. I took very little money for doing it, but that was how I got my start. I was 20 years old before I got the opportunity to drive a racecar.

Dale Jarrett with his dad, Ned, and his son, Jason.

The one thing my dad stressed to me was for me to learn my business and that meant working on the cars. I think that's probably been the best advice. Dad also told me from a young age and still tells me to this day, "Treat other people how you want to be treated yourself." That has always stuck with me and helped me throughout my career.

My father and I talk after each and every race. He's the one person I can always count on for advice. Not only does he have the insight of being in championship battles himself, but through his TV and radio work, he's seen over the years what different drivers have gone through in trying to win the Winston Cup Championship. Dad's always been a great support system, but especially this past year, he's helped me handle the pressure and tried to make it all run as smoothly as possible. It's great to have a father who's there for me week in and week out.

I grew up basically in the same county in North Carolina that I live in now, so I see a lot of the same things happening with our family that I did growing up around the sport. I'm trying to instill in my kids the same solid values that Dad taught me. He was—and is—a good family person who was also a champion at what he did. My father is a great dad and I'm very fortunate.

◆ Dale Jarrett is the son of NASCAR great, Ned Jarrett. He is the 1999 NASCAR Winston Cup Series Champion and has won the Daytona 500, NASCAR's most prestigious race, three times.

Franklin Raines

Chairman and CEO, Fannie Mae

MY FATHER WAS A JANITOR FOR THE CITY OF SEATTLE AND HE HAD A PRETTY hard life. Not only did he have seven children to raise, he also suffered a number of medical problems. But he took on all of these obligations that he had and he stuck to them. By watching him, I learned the value of perseverance. I don't think he ever thought that he achieved that much in his life. But I know he did. He sent a number of his kids to college, built a family home by hand, and sent us all into the world with as much opportunity as could ever have been expected.

My father didn't graduate from high school and my mother went through just primary school. Consequently, education was not a central part of their lives. I think my father would have loved to have gone on to college, but when he was growing up he was not in a financial position to do so. Because of this experience, education was stressed in our household. Mom and Dad always encouraged us to go to school and do well. They even stretched their budget in order to buy us a set of encyclopedias. They made certain that we were involved in every aspect of school.

My father was never a very touchy-feely person. But the day before I went off to Harvard on a full scholarship, Dad pulled me aside.

"Watch out for yourself," he said.

That's about as loquacious as he would get. He had no idea what college was like—let alone what Harvard was about. He just wanted me to know that he was concerned about me. That quiet way typified him. It only took a few words from him to let me know that he was thinking about me.

You would have to know my father to appreciate how proud he could be of my accomplishments. It took some type of external validation for him to really put things in perspective. When I came back from my first semester at college, I put a Harvard sticker on the back of his station wagon. It only became very meaningful for him when his co-workers reacted to it. Dad didn't know where Harvard fit in the whole galaxy of things, but when he saw how impressed his friends were, then his chest would puff out.

He was also very proud when I was nominated as budget director for the Clinton administration. But through all of my successes, I think in his mind he was thinking, "Frank is doing all these things and I don't know quite what they are." Occasionally he would ask, "What do you actually do?" or "What is an investment banker?" He may not have always understood what I did, but I could tell he was proud of me.

My dad instilled in me certain values that are still important to me

(Photo Credit: Sam Kittner, Courtesy of Fannie Mae.)

Franklin Raines.

today—loyalty, responsibility, and perseverance. When he built the family home, he literally dug the foundation by hand. He then bought an old house that was going to be torn down by the highway department. Over a period of five years, he dismantled it piece by piece and used the lumber to build the house. He simply had this dream and he persevered in seeking it over a very long period of time.

It's a little hard for me to complain about certain things now when I grew up seeing real hardships and saw what my father went through. He just never gave up. That encouraged me to give 100 percent to every endeavor throughout my life—just like he did.

My father had many responsibilities growing up and there were times when he would get depressed about his heavy load. But what made him so special was that he would rally and go back to it. He would have liked to have had an easier life, but he took the cards that he was dealt and did the best he could with them. I appreciate everything he did.

◆ Franklin Raines is the chairman and CEO of Fannie Mae. He previously served as th director of the Office of Management and Budget for the Clinton administration

Tom Dolan

Olympic Gold Medalist, 400 IM Swimming

WHEN I WAS YOUNG, I PLAYED A LOT OF DIFFERENT SPORTS. IN ADDITION TO swimming, I played basketball, baseball, soccer, golf, and tennis. My parents encouraged me to try all these sports so that I could see what was out there and figure out what I liked and what I didn't like. Dad stressed to my sister and me to have fun in whatever we did. He used to tell me, "You can compete all you want and work as hard as you want to win. But only do it as long as you're having fun." It sounds like a simple message, but it can be easy to forget—particularly at my level of swimming. There was never any pressure for me to continue swimming just because that's where I was the most successful. He always felt that I should be doing what interested me.

Growing up, the main thing that I really appreciated was how my dad was always there for me. He supported all of my athletic endeavors, but that support never crossed the line of applying pressure. He used to have a saying for me when I was 10 years old and it still holds true today: "No matter what happens tomorrow—even if you break a leg or something happens where you can never swim again—you've done more than most people can even dream about." He was very good at putting things into perspective. I never really needed too much spurring on, because my competitive nature is a part of who I am. I hate to lose and I'll do everything I can not to lose. But I think for him, it was all about me competing in activities for the right reasons and having fun while doing them.

About two months before the Olympic trials in 1996, I came down with chronic fatigue syndrome, which basically stemmed from over-training. I had worked so hard that I had gotten to the point where my body wasn't recovering at night. I would wake up in the morning and my heart rate would be three to four times higher than it should be. Basically, my body was never resting. As a result, we went to see more doctors than I can remember. It got to the point where the medical consensus was for me to stay off my feet, rest as much as possible, and just swim very slowly and very easily.

This prescription from the doctors couldn't have come at a worse time. With the swimming trials just a month and a half away, now was not the time to slow down. I wanted to make the Olympic team in multiple events. My dad took the news a lot better than I did. He saw this bad luck as a challenge that we would work through together. Every weekend he'd fly from Washington to Ann Arbor, Michigan, to meet with the doctors that I was seeing, to meet with my coach and to see me. He wanted me to relax and wanted to put me at ease. Those weekends meant a lot to me. It took a tremendous amount of pressure off my back to know that he supported me so much. By the time the trials arrived in March, my body had recovered. I swam great at the trials and was able to win a gold medal at the Olympics.

For him, this support was second nature. In his mind, there was never a question about whether he'd fly every weekend to be with me. He told me, "We're going to fix this thing and that's the end of the story." The way

(Photo courtesy of Tom Dolan)

Tom Dolan with his dad, Bill (circa 1999).

he handled that situation was so typical of my dad and I know that it had a huge impact on what happened to me at the Olympics.

There are swimmers that I have looked up to for their work ethic or other athletes whom I have admired. But my dad is my hero. Ever since I was a little kid, I always looked up to my dad as the one true hero that I have in the world.

◆ Tom Dolan won a gold medal in the 400-meter individual medley swimming event at the 1996 Summer Olympics in Atlanta. He holds the world record in this event and continues training for the 2000 Olympic Games in Sydney, Australia.

Jim Cramer

Founder, The Street.com

MY FATHER HAS ALWAYS BEEN INCREDIBLY HARD-WORKING AND HE encouraged me to do as well as possible in school. In fourth grade, I brought home a sub-par report card from Mrs. Turoff's class at Hartwell Lane Elementary School. My father said this was inexcusable and became very angry. He told me I could do much better. I remember this so well because I was fighting back tears. But boy, did this motivate me!

Dad wasn't the type of father who was quick to offer praise—even when I did well. Instead he often told me, "Jim, you can do more." That's what made it problematic for me. I was at the top of my class in high school. I was the top of my class at college. I was the editor-in-chief of the college newspaper. But still, my father felt I could do more. As a result, I always felt like I was letting him down. I finished eighth in the Government Department at Harvard, and while that may be impressive, it also meant that there were seven people who were better than I was.

At times, I thought that there was too much pressure on me to do well. When I was in my twenties, I thought that I grew up in a house that was too strict and too focused. After I got into Harvard Law School, I actually didn't want to tell my dad because I didn't want to make him feel so happy about all the pushing that he gave me!

But as I entered my thirties, I realized that I was able to accomplish a lot of things in my life because my father thought that I could always do better. I think that he toughened me mentally and I love him for that.

In high school, I was captain of my soccer team. I regarded team sports as being fabulous. Dad saw it as a waste of time. While my mom was at every one of my games, Dad had a small business to run. I think my father would have loved to have been at some of those games. But at the time, that's not what dads did. Dads worked. But within the context of how hard my dad worked, he paid a massive amount of attention to me. What he did was prepare me for life. My father raised me to be an ethical, successful person and businessman.

He instilled in me the value of honesty. There was a right and wrong in my house that was almost Old Testament–like in how I was supposed to do things. I never was late with a library book. I never missed a day of school. I never got involved in drugs. He also taught me to have a work ethic that I wish others had. I didn't really understand how important it was until I went out on my own and started running a business.

People often say, "Jim, you have this hedge fund business and now you have The Street.com. How do you balance everything?"

And I always say, "This is a lot easier than when I was growing up!"

Even though Dad still lives down in Philadelphia, I see him all the time. Does he wish that he had praised me more when I was growing up? Well, he's made up for it in spades by telling me now anytime I do a good job that I've done a good job. He even came up to New York to be with me when The Street.com went public—just to tell me how proud he was of me. People change. He's also figured out the praise thing for his grandchildren. And that's fantastic. I love it. And I love him.

◆ Jim Cramer is the founder of TheStreet.com, the manager of a hedge fund, and a regular commentator on CNBC.

(Photo courtesy of Jim Cramer)

Jim Cramer and his dad, Ken (circa 1998).

Scott Karl

Pitcher, Colorado Rockies

I THINK THAT BECAUSE OF WHAT MY DAD DOES FOR A LIVING, MY SISTER AND
I learned early on the difference between right and wrong. He's a
correctional officer for the state of California and his job often meant
moves to various prisons in the southern part of the state.

Dad kept us removed from what he does. He left behind any negative
feelings that were derived from his work. I know he saw some pretty
rough individuals down at the prison, but he never brought that home.
The only things he brought home were the values of the hard work, right
and wrong, and those things that can help an individual grow.

Dad set the rules and we knew that as long as we abided by them, we
could just be kids. But we also knew that if we crossed the line, we
definitely would pay the consequences.

I remember in high school, I was in auto shop class and I was trying
to fix my own car. Because I couldn't get it fixed in time, I ditched a
couple of my classes. When Dad received a report about those absences
at home, he asked me about it. Instead of telling him the reason I cut
those classes, I basically lied to him. Dad's reaction was to lay down the
law. He took my car away for awhile, but also explained why he was
punishing me.

"Scott, you really screwed up," he said. "But let's just try to work back
to where we had been."

He was compassionate with his discipline—strict but very fair. That's
just an example of pure love as far as I am concerned between a father
and a son.

One of the great things about my dad's job was that he was often able
to set his own schedule. This allowed him to come out to my games,
whether they were on a Saturday or fell in the middle of the week. For a
few years, he even coached my little league teams. Growing up, Dad was
very supportive and encouraging of everything that I did.

One of the most important things I learned from my father was the ability to relax and stay evenly keeled. He always said, "Whether things are going well or not going well, you need to maintain your emotions. This will allow you to be able to respond under pressure."

Consequently, I act the same whether I'm on a five-game winning streak or a five-game losing streak. I don't let the circumstances dictate my emotions.

Growing up, I probably lost my cool a few times and blew my concentration. But for the most part, I held it together pretty well. Dad instilled this focus in me and it has helped tremendously at the major league level. We play so many games, and if I rode this emotional roller coaster, I think it would end up driving me crazy!

Dad has always been my number one fan and was very supportive of my decision to leave college early after I was drafted. He saw my talent as a pitcher develop at the University of Hawaii and knew I had the discipline to reach my full potential. It has always been a dream of mine to pitch in the major leagues and Dad has always encouraged me to pursue my goals. He also knew that if I realized over time that I just

(Photo courtesy of Scott Karl)

Scott Karl with his dad, Gene (circa 1997).

wasn't good enough, that I would certainly go back and finish my education.

My parents rounded up a whole bunch of family members to come out to see me pitch during my first trip to the West Coast. I think they were more nervous than I was! Since then, they've seen me play at just about every major league field.

I've always seen my dad as a super strong individual and a great role model. I'm proud that I've made it to the majors. But if I can grow up and have kids and raise them just as my dad raised me, I'll think of that as a great accomplishment.

◆ Scott Karl is a starting pitcher for the Colorado Rockies.

William Kennard

Chairman, FCC

MY FATHER'S NAME WAS ROBERT KENNARD AND HE WAS THE SINGLE GREATEST influence in my life. He was an architect who started his own business the year I was born. At that time in Los Angeles it was very difficult for an African-American architect to have his own business. I remember very distinctly when he would come home from work and tell us about the difficulties he had trying to get new business. People told him flat out, "You can't be an African-American architect and have your own business. You've got to work for somebody white." But Dad just persevered. He said, "I'm going to show them. I'm going to demonstrate that this can be done." Ultimately he built the oldest continuously operated African-American architectural firm in the West.

I learned to persevere in life by following my dad's example. When he was five years old and there was de-facto segregation in Los Angeles, his parents sent him off to the school closest to home. It was the neighborhood school—but it also happened to be the white school. On his first day, the principal told him, "You can't go to this school." He sent him home and then called my grandmother and told her that my dad would have to go to the Negro school several miles away. The next day, my grandparents dressed my father up again and sent him back to the neighborhood school. The principal again sent him right back home. This went on for many days. Finally my grandparents sat my father down and they said, "This is your neighborhood, this is your school, and this is where you deserve to go." Eventually they brought the matter to the school board and the school system relented.

The moral of the story, as my father explained it was this, "If you believe in something and you believe you're right and you keep fighting, you will succeed." It became the rallying cry for all of us.

Dad wasn't the sort of father that made me feel like I was being pushed. Instead, I always felt like I was being counseled. He never told me,

"I want you to succeed," or "I want you to be successful." He would always ask me first, "What do you want?" He told me that I could accomplish anything in life as long as I was willing to work for it.

My father was very proud of my accomplishments all throughout my life. He would never tell me, though. But when I would hear him talk to his friends or our relatives about his kids, there was a great sense of pride in his voice.

I remember on his 70th birthday, my two older sisters and I threw a big party for him. We had a lot of his friends and family over. It was a pretty big deal. Many of his friends got up and talked about how great his kids were and what a great accomplishment it was that all of his children went to Stanford, got professional degrees, and were very successful. When my father stood up he said, "You know, I'm really proud of my children and I'm proud of their accomplishments, but I'm most proud of the fact they all are friends and love each other and love us. That," he said, "was the most important thing that I feel I've accomplished."

There are two values that my dad taught me that are really important to me today. One was community. My father felt that if you had the

(Photo courtesy of William Kennard)

William Kennard and his family (with dad, Robert).

privilege of getting an education and being able to have a profession, that you had to give back to your community. He taught me that it's not enough to have a successful career. "Your success," he said, "is defined by how you weave your work into the fabric of building your community." His way of giving back was by physically rebuilding communities. He loved to design things like churches, synagogues, schools, and community centers because that was the way communities came together.

The other value that was instilled in me was the value of multiculturalism. My father saw a vision of this country as being one of diversity and tolerance for other people. Throughout our lives, my parents insisted that we always lived in integrated environments. Dad made sure that we grew up in a neighborhood that had lots of different people. I went to one of the most diverse high schools in Los Angeles, where we had students from the Far East and the Middle East, Central and South America. To this day, people joke that my group of friends resembles the U.N.!

I always knew what my father did for a living. When I was a young boy, my father and I would sometimes drive around Los Angeles on a Saturday and he would point out to me the scores of buildings that he designed. We would even go in the buildings. We'd put hard-hats on, walk around a project of his, and he'd tell me how certain building elements were accomplished. On the walls in my office are pictures of the buildings that he designed. They're really monuments to what he accomplished in his life.

My father passed away in March of 1995. But the testimony that my father left behind is not just in the buildings that he built, but also in the people that he touched. He meant so much to so many people.

◆ William Kennard is the chairman of the Federal Communications Commission.

Franklin Graham

President, Samaritan's Purse

IT NEVER DAWNED ON ME AS I WAS GROWING UP THAT MY FATHER WAS WELL known. He was just my father. I wasn't with him when he met the Queen of England or when he visited President Eisenhower at the White House. But I remember one day when I was nine years old, a friend of his who worked for the local utility company flew my dad home in a helicopter. He landed it in our front yard in Montreat, North Carolina, and I realized that there was something a little unusual about this. Most fathers don't arrive home in a helicopter!

A year later, I went to his crusade in New York's Madison Square Garden. I saw the thousands of people who had come to see my father. I came to understand that my dad was indeed different.

The Billy Graham that the world saw in public was the same man that we saw at home in private. There weren't two Billy Grahams. My father lived what he said. He didn't say one thing and then live another life. He walked the talk. His integrity and his faithfulness to the gospel of Jesus Christ have always been a part of who he is—twenty-four hours a day, seven days a week.

I've never heard him use a slang word. I've never heard him use the word, "Darn." Or say, "Oh shoot." In fact, I've never heard him say anything that was off-color. I've been in his presence when people have said a joke that would perhaps be suggestive sexually or maybe would have racial overtones, but I've never even seen my father crack a smile. He would never even acknowledge to the person who was telling the joke that it was funny or appeared to be funny. My father would just glare at him. And, of course, they got the hint real quick that Billy Graham doesn't put up with stuff like that. So my father has just always been a straight arrow.

I appreciate that more as an adult maybe than I did when I was younger. All these years he's never detoured. He's been very careful not to allow things to sidetrack him from what he felt God called him to do.

The example that he set in the home mirrored his own spiritual values. We never started the day without Bible reading and a short time of prayer. We never ended the day without Bible reading and a time of prayer. We always prayed on our knees as a family. My father also never made devotions boring. He always kept them short and simple so we, as children, wouldn't lose our attention. This is also what he's done when he preaches on the pulpit. He always delivers his message in such a way that the common person can understand what he's saying. I think that's one of my father's greatest gifts. He's been able to keep the truth of God's word simple.

I don't think my life was much different than any other kid growing up in the sixties on rock 'n' roll. I was a normal teenager. I never got into the drug scene. That held no interest for me. But alcohol and girls were a different story. People would expect me—being the son of Billy Graham— to maybe walk around with a Bible under my arm. But just because I'm the son of Billy Graham doesn't mean I have any special favor with God. It doesn't matter who your parents are or who your family is. We're all sinners before God.

(Photo courtesy of Samaritan's Purse.)

Franklin Graham and his dad, Dr. Billy Graham.

When I came home and told my father I had been expelled from college, he was not a happy camper. I can tell you that! But at the same time, my parents continued to love me and continued to accept me. They didn't hold it over my head. They tried to encourage me to pick up and go forward.

Despite my parents' support, I didn't want God in my life. I didn't want his son, Jesus Christ, in my life. I wanted to party and have fun and live by my rules. But there was an emptiness in my life. Something was missing. And what it was, was a relationship with God in my life. At the age of 22, I got on my knees and asked for God's forgiveness. I accepted his provision for my sin—his son Jesus Christ.

My father let me find my spirituality in my own way and in my own time. I think he realized that there was only so much he could do as a parent. But he set the example. Unfortunately many times parents do not set the example. They'll tell their kids, "Don't do drugs." But they'll turn around and open up the liquor cabinet and have their martinis and their screwdrivers. Kids, meanwhile, are saying to themselves, "Well you've got your drugs, why can't I have mine?" My parents set the example at home. And I think it's really important—especially today—that parents be role models for their children.

My father never put pressure on me to follow in his footsteps. Never. Several times he said, "If God ever called you to be a preacher, I would be proud." But I never felt any pressure to do this. I never went to seminary. The thing my father was concerned about was my spiritual life, and he realized my rebellion growing up stemmed from a spiritual need in my life. Until I asked Jesus Christ to come into my heart and come into my life, I would continue to have these problems. He just prayed for me and loved me.

Love was always present in our home. I can never remember my parents having a fight. Now as an adult, I know that in the past they have had strong disagreements. But they never did it in front of the children. They would go lock the door in the bedroom and then have it out. But in front of the children, they were always united. I was probably in my twenties before I realized that they had had fights! It was just so important for them to show that kind of love and that kind of respect for one another in the home.

I've always admired my dad and I always appreciated the integrity in his life. My father didn't put up with too much foolishness from us. He could be a strong disciplinarian. But at the same time, we respected him because we knew he was honest. We knew that when he said something, it was true and that he wasn't a man of double standards. He was and is a true role model.

◆ Franklin Graham is the president of Samaritan's Purse, an international Christian relief agency, and is the first vice chairman of the Billy Graham Evangelistic Association.

Eric Lindros

Captain, Philadelphia Flyers

ALTHOUGH MY DAD WAS VERY BUSY AS A PUBLIC ACCOUNTANT, HE ALWAYS seemed to be around when I was growing up. As a result, my brother, sister, and I never felt neglected in any way. When I was 10 years old, we moved to Toronto from London, Ontario. Dad knew how much I loved to play hockey, so he took out the concrete swimming pool and each winter made an ice rink in the backyard. We played there all the time. Dad even organized practices for my friends at the local arena, where he would run us through a series of drills for an hour or so. He really loved to be with us and never saw it as a chore.

Dad would often say, "Nothing in life comes easy." He taught me the value of hard work. In hockey, there are always going to be difficult times and I've had more than my share. When I was 14, I grew about seven inches in the course of eight months. I was as awkward as a baby calf out on the ice. There were times when my frustration would be so great, that I considered quitting. But my dad told me to be patient and to stick with it. He encouraged me and instilled me with confidence at a time when I really needed it.

As I improved in my abilities, Dad did everything he could to help me pursue a sport that I loved very much. He'd take me just about anywhere to play a game. Because Toronto is so spread out, sometimes he'd drive me an hour and a half just to play in a 50-minute game. Then we'd get back in the station wagon for the long drive home. The running joke at home was that Dad had become a professional carpool driver! He was just so dedicated to my interests and the interests of my brother and sister. I never had any doubt about my dad's support.

Despite my obvious attachment to hockey, my parents always made sure that I had other interests. Education, for instance, was very important in our family—we had to have good grades or we couldn't play. Dad also taught me to take a big picture approach to life. "Hockey is great," he said.

"It's a lot of fun. It is what you love to do. But there's a lot of life out there as well."

After my experience last year with my collapsed lung, I began to see that a lot of what he had said to me growing up was beginning to kick in and make sense.

My father stepped into a new world when, at my request, he became my full-time agent. This meant stepping away from a partnership in Canada's largest accounting firm and a job where he was very successful and admired by his peers. I know it was a tough pill for him to swallow—particularly with the controversy that surrounded me when I entered the NHL. Dad has been accused of some terrible things by the media. This has made me realize that everything that appears on TV and in the newspaper isn't always what it appears to be. Still, it is always difficult to read something negative about your father—especially when I know what a good and special person he is.

◆ Eric Lindros, an all-star center, is the captain of the Philadelphia Flyers.

(Photo courtesy of Quality Bound Limited)

Eric Lindros with his parents.

Swoosie Kurtz

Actor

My dad retired from the Air Force after a career that included the command of three Flying Fortress Groups composed of thousands of men and hundreds of bombers. He was a pioneer of jet aviation. When strangers met him, they expected him to be a strict, gruff disciplinarian. They figured that a legendary military man who was a war hero had to be like the "Great Santini." Well, Frankie, as I called him, could not have been further from that image. He was sweet, gentle, and soft-spoken. He was also very self-deprecating. I know that he was a strong leader with his men when lives depended on him. But he was never tough with me—ever. I was an only child and was the center of his universe.

(Photo courtesy of Swoosie Kurtz)

Swoosie Kurtz, her dad, Col. Frank Kurtz, and his plane, "The Swoose."

In my early years of high school, my father retired from the military and we moved to Los Angeles. Frankie decided that now was a good time to enter the business world. I had heard of this legendary drama teacher at Hollywood High School, but because we moved after the school year had begun, the class was already filled. This teacher was very popular and everyone wanted to be in his class. I was just heartbroken and I cried. When my father got home from work I was still sobbing. I tried to explain to him what was wrong.

"I know this man is great and I want to study with him," I said. "This is all I want to do in life."

Frankie put his arm around me and said, "Well, we'll just find a way. There's always an answer." My dad was always like this. He always believed there was a solution to every problem—even when it looked impossible. The next day, instead of going to work, he drove to Hollywood High and spoke to the principal and the drama teacher. He explained to them my passion for acting and theater and the fact that we had moved into town after the class had been filled. Whatever he said worked. The next day, I began my first drama class at Hollywood High.

He was never afraid to ask for anything. His attitude was, "Of course they're going to say no, but it doesn't hurt to ask." "No" for him was just the beginning—especially as it related to me. Even though he came from a background of self-discipline, he felt that rules are sometimes meant to be broken.

If there was something I wanted to do, my dad supported me 100 percent. He never questioned what I wanted or why I wanted it. It was a huge confidence-builder and it gave me a great foundation growing up. Frankie also told me to never, ever rest on your laurels. He never did. He never spent any time congratulating himself and basking in whatever he had accomplished. He would simply move on to the next mission or the next project. I can see this in myself. I am very proud of my past performances and my awards and the roles I have created, but that's history to me. I'm only interested in what's going on now and what's going to happen down the road.

Rejection is a part of my business. It's still tough, but it's particularly hard when you're just starting out. It can be quite discouraging. I can remember when I was in my early twenties reading for a part that I really wanted. After several call-backs I felt I was so close, but the producers ended up going with somebody else. I was very down. But my dad found a way to pull me out of discouragement and keep me from giving up. He said, "Don't take your eyes off the horizon. Compete with yourself. Run your own race." He was such a cockeyed optimist and he had an incredible amount of confidence in me.

When "Sisters" began on NBC, he was thrilled. He called me up to talk about the show and said, "This is going to run for five years!" I sarcastically replied, "Yeah, right."

After we were renewed for our last season—our fifth—I said, "Well, Frankie, I got to hand it to you. You were right."

The day that he died, or "made his last flight," as we call it, the first words out of my mouth were, "Thank you, Frankie, for everything." He gave me so much. I really think my whole career as an actress, my work ethic, my concentration, and my focus came from him. He was one of my best friends throughout my life and I feel very blessed to have had him for a father.

◆ Swoosie Kurtz is one of America's preeminent comedic and dramatic actors. She is an Emmy Award winner, and a recipient of two Tony Awards. Her distinctive name, given to her by the press, comes from the B-17 Flying Fortress, "The Swoose," which now resides in the Smithsonian Air & Space Museum. The airplane was flown by her father, Col. Frank Kurtz, who was the most decorated Air Force pilot of World War II.

Peter Coors

CEO, Coors Brewing Company

I REALLY DIDN'T THINK ABOUT WHETHER I WOULD ENTER THE "FAMILY BUSINESS" while I was growing up in the '50s and the '60s. The business certainly didn't have the presence that it has today. Back then, Coors was only in 11 Western states and very few people in the East had actually heard of the company!

When I was very young, Dad used to bring me down to the brewery with my brothers on Saturdays to walk around and tour the place. At a very young age I observed the friendly and warm relationship that Dad had with the employees. He had tremendous respect for them and what they do.

I spent my summers working in various jobs at the plant—mechanic, pipe fitter, and a number of production jobs. I think the one thing that kind of put it all in perspective for me was after I graduated with an engineering degree and an MBA, my first job with Coors was as a trainee in our waste treatment plant. There was no favoritism. The family philosophy has always been that this is not a business for the family; this is a family for the business.

My father raised me in a pretty conservative manner. By any measure, we didn't have an ostentatious lifestyle. Dad always wanted the best for us without giving it to us. Growing up, no matter how bad I wanted something, I either had to earn it or wait for it. Dad taught me that things have value and that I had to be patient.

When I needed a car, I used the family car, which was an old Chevy. I was finally able to get a car in my sophomore year in college. As a high school graduation present, Dad gave me enough money to buy half the car I wanted. Between work and investing the money, I was able to raise the remainder. By waiting to get a car, Dad taught me discipline and responsibility. I learned that when you have to wait awhile for something, it makes you appreciate it that much more.

One of the things he always used to say was, "You don't have to be right all the time." Now Dad was very successful and I admired him greatly for both his academic achievements and his success at his business. But I once asked him, "How does anybody ever get to be that smart and do that well?"

Dad put his arm around me, leaned into me and in a stage whisper said, "Well, you don't see the mistakes I make. You've just got to realize that you've got to make more right decisions than you make bad decisions and you'll get along just fine. Just do your best."

One of the things I valued very much growing up was that we always had family dinner together. It was always at six thirty. Dad would come home at five thirty, read the paper a little bit, check in on what we had done for the day, and then sit down at the dinner table. It was just a great opportunity for all of us to sit around and talk about what was going on in our lives and what was going on in the world.

The only thing that Dad ever really got mad at us about was when we got our mom upset. It usually occurred

(Photo Credit: David Topping Photography. Courtesy of Coors Brewing Company)

Peter Coors with his dad, Joseph.

when one of my brothers and I got into a fight. We couldn't get our passion under control and she couldn't get her passion under control. When she got to her wit's end and couldn't stand it anymore, she would call Dad at the brewery and tell him to come home. This was the worst thing that could possibly happen. The brewery was in eyesight of our house and it didn't take too long for him to get there. At times like this, it usually meant a pretty good spanking. We knew that when he was home in the middle of the day we were in really big trouble! Through the years, under my father's tutelage, I came to appreciate that level of respect and caring that children should have for their parents.

Four-generation family businesses aren't all that normal. But I think one of the main reasons Coors continues to thrive is because of the strong values that have been passed on to each generation. I learned so much from my father and I teach my six children a lot of what I learned from my dad.

◆Peter Coors is vice chairman and CEO of the Coors Brewing Company in Golden, Colorado. His father Joseph remains vice chairman of the Adolph Coors Company.

Roberto Alomar

Second Baseman, Cleveland Indians

I GREW UP IN A BASEBALL FAMILY. MY DAD WAS A BASEBALL PLAYER AND practically everyone in his family were baseball players. Despite this family history, he never pushed me to follow in his footsteps. Instead, he just let me do whatever I wanted to do. I played basketball and soccer growing up in Puerto Rico, but, in the end, I saw that I had a great ability to play the game of baseball. Besides, seeing my dad play all those years in the big leagues made me want to emulate him. That's one of the main reasons I chose to play the game.

Dad has always told me to play hard, to give 100 percent, and to do the best I can. He used to say, "Baseball is a team sport and if you give anything less than your best, you not only let yourself down, but also your team."

As I participated in athletics from an early age and developed certain talents in baseball, Dad took me aside and taught me to also respect others. He said, "Your gifts are very special and others may not possess what you have. But it's important to respect them and appreciate the fact that they too are giving their best." This had a big impact on me.

Dad taught me by example. He talked to me and showed me the right way to do things. He never screamed at me or raised his hand in anger. He is a very patient person. That's why he works so well with young players.

When my brother and I started playing, I was seven. Dad suggested that I start switch hitting. He said, "If you want to be an everyday player, that would be the easiest way to play every day." I think that was great advice. I wasn't good at hitting on my right side immediately. But he worked with me every day until I felt comfortable. Now, of course, I am a switch hitter and he helped me so much along the way. His patience paid off for me in a big way.

Dad has also given me lessons about life. From an early age, Dad taught me to just be who I am. I'm more of a quiet person and sometimes—particularly in baseball—my sense of purpose and introspection could be perceived as a certain jadedness or complacency. But Dad said, "If you always give 100 percent in everything that you do, people will come to respect you." He's taught me everything that I know. He taught me discipline, he taught me right from wrong, and he taught me to make the most of the talent that God has given me. But perhaps the best thing my dad ever did was what he didn't do. He never pushed me to be a ballplayer.

I still remember when I came up to the big leagues with San Diego in 1988. It was a very special day for me and my dad. I was going up in the escalators in Dodger Stadium and my father was there waiting for me in the lobby of the clubhouse. Dad was my coach. It was a huge thrill. Not only had I achieved my goal of making it to the big leagues, but

(Photo courtesy of the Cleveland Indians)

Roberto Alomar and his family (including his dad, Sandy, Sr., mom, Maria, brother, Sandy Jr., and sister, Sandia).

one of my coaches when I finally got there was my dad. It is something that I will never forget. He helped me a lot in my first year, which is typically a ballplayer's toughest year. I know that without my dad's guidance growing up, I would never be the person that I am today.

My dad has always been my hero and always been my idol. Even though I'm in the big leagues now and he's not up here with me, I still talk to him on a regular basis. He gives me good advice about baseball and about life.

◆ Roberto Alomar is the all-star second baseman for the Cleveland Indians.

J.W. "Bill" Marriott, Jr.

Chairman and CEO—Marriott International, Inc.

IN TERMS OF A ROLE MODEL, MY FATHER WAS PROBABLY THE MOST IMPORTANT figure in my life. He set a great example of hard work, dedication to the church, and dedication to his family.

He was a tough businessman and in many ways, he was also a tough father. But I think that toughness strengthened me and helped me in the business world.

Although my father was very busy growing up, I always knew that he loved me and cared about me. The reason is that he paid attention to the results. He was worried about my school work, he was concerned about my education, and he made a point of inspecting the work from my chores. If we didn't mow the lawn or wash the car right the first time, my brother and I would do it again. He was very concerned that we did things right and that we learned from our mistakes.

We never went to church in a dirty car. If we came out to go to church on Sunday morning in our Sunday finest and the car was not clean, we'd wash the car and get our clothes dirty. We'd be late for church, but we'd go to church in a clean car. My dad was a perfectionist even when it came to the most trivial things. Later on in life, when he visited my family at our house we actually went through a mini-inspection! He made sure that we had the floors clean in the kitchen and that none of the children's clothes were lying on the floor. He was also very concerned about my children's appearance.

He built the business that way. He insisted that all of his restaurants and hotels had to be in absolute perfect order. There was no second best or third best. It had to absolutely be the best or it wasn't satisfactory. My father was the ultimate hands-on manager. He visited his restaurants almost every day, often with my younger brother Dick and me in tow. Of course, as a kid, I just thought we were going out to eat. As I got older, I caught on to what Dad was up to. To him, the best way—the only way—to know what was really going on in his business was to see it and hear it with his own eyes and ears.

Despite his striving for perfection, he was very patient and instructive if someone made a mistake. He would sometimes give a couple of harsh words to straighten out what needed to be done, but then he would put his arm around the employee and tell them how much they meant to the company. He would always leave people feeling good about themselves and about him. That's why he was so respected.

(Photo courtesy of Marriott International, Inc.)

Dad was very concerned about his employees' welfare and well-being. Back in the '30s, he hired a doctor full time to take care of his employees before there were any healthcare plans in corporate America. He even hired a surgeon to operate on them in the early '40s. He was very paternalistic and his people loved him. They'd go to

J.W. ("Bill") Marriott, Jr., with his dad, J.W. Marriott, Sr.

the end of the earth for him. This concern that he had for his employees had a tremendous impact on me. Dad taught me how to work, he taught me the importance of work, and he taught me the importance of treating everyone with respect.

What made my dad so successful was his love of work, his quest for perfection, his attention to detail, and the love he had—and showed—for his employees. He also had a desire to continuously improve. He used to say to me, "Success is never final." He borrowed this phrase from Churchill, but he really believed that. He believed that you had to go out every day and improve on what you had done the day before. His life was one of constant and continuous improvement both for himself and for his family.

◆ J.W. "Bill" Marriott, Jr. is the chairman and CEO of Marriott International, Inc., which has hotels in 50 states and 25 countries.

Floyd Mayweather, Jr.

WBC Super Featherweight Champion

WHEN I WAS IN THE SECOND GRADE IN GRAND RAPIDS, MICHIGAN, I BULLIED other students in school on a fairly regular basis. I was a bully despite my small size. In fact, I was the smallest guy in my class.

One day it was raining very hard and my dad drove me to school. He would often do this so I didn't have to wait for a school bus in the rain. On this particular day, I forgot my raincoat. When we got to school he dropped me off, wished me a good day, and then drove away. I forgot that he was going to come back to school to bring me my raincoat. That was bad luck on my part because I bumped into my father as I was chasing a kid out of class. He wasn't too pleased. He said, "I'm going to see you when you get home."

When I came home from school, Dad was waiting for me. He gave me a whooping I'll never forget. He then told me, "You better straighten up in school. I don't want to see you acting up or even hear about it."

It was a tremendous learning experience on my part. Even though my dad punished me, it meant a lot to me to know that my dad cared about me and my behavior toward others. Most of my friends' fathers weren't even there for their sons. My dad always was and is still there for me today. He's been there for me through thick and thin. When I was sick he took care of me. When I played football, he came to all of my games and supported me. He always taught me right from wrong and taught me from an early age to show respect to other people.

From an early age, Dad stressed the value of a dollar. He'd tell me, "Money doesn't grow on trees." The idea was that if I had a family someday, and if anything happened to me, my family would be well off and well taken care of. He taught me this lesson from personal experience. My dad had a lot of money at one time. But he blew a lot of it on senseless things. He's been down the hard road and he doesn't want me to travel down there.

Normally when people go to jail, you write each other letters. But when my father was sent to jail for conspiracy in a drug case, I would visit him almost every day. Even from behind bars, Dad instilled in me the right values. He didn't want me to end up where he was at that particular time—which was prison. Thankfully, Dad's out of jail now and we're a family again. I owe my World Championship to him. He has devoted all of his time to me.

My dad is my hero. He's always supported me 100 percent and given me a lot of confidence to be the best in the world. If my dad wasn't always looking out for me and always on my back, I don't think I'd be where I am today. He's everything to me and I love him with all my heart.

(Photo Credit: Chris Farina (1995). Courtesy of Top Rank.)

Floyd Mayweather, Jr. with his dad, Floyd Mayweather, Sr.

◆ Floyd Mayweather, Jr. is the WBC Super Featherweight Champion of the World.

Wally Szczerbiak

Forward, Minnesota Timberwolves

My dad was drafted to play basketball in the United States after graduating from college, but he didn't quite make it. He had some tough luck and he got cut by a couple of teams. Finally, he was offered a one-year guaranteed contract by the Buffalo Braves. But he turned that down to play for a team in Madrid that offered him a five-year guaranteed contract. He took the security in Europe over the prestige of the NBA, and he ended up having a great career overseas.

The only way to describe my dad is that he does everything right. The way he has raised me has been the way he has run his own life. He has a very good heart and is an extremely good-natured person. He has always strived to give me the best advice and he has raised me in the best moral way. That's pretty much how he's been as a father all along.

I've playing sports throughout my life. I started off playing soccer quite a bit when I was younger. In fourth grade I moved on to basketball. All along my dad just allowed me to go do whatever it was I really enjoyed. He never pushed me in any particular direction. But once he saw I had a love for basketball, he would play with me whenever I asked him to. And that's the main reason I got very good at it.

My dad left the decision about where I would attend college and play basketball completely up to me. He felt that was the best way to do it. He didn't want to influence me. Instead, he wanted me to make the decision from the bottom of my heart. He helped me here and there, but in the end, I chose Miami because I really felt comfortable there. My dad obviously had a lot of confidence in me because it ended up working out really well.

When I was a freshman in college I started beating my dad at one-on-one. I think he was very happy and proud that I had improved so much as a player. But at the same time, he's a competitive guy with an ego. And he saw that he was kind of going downhill and I was going in the opposite direction. That wasn't easy for him. He didn't say anything, but I could just tell.

My dad instilled in me from an early age that I should live life the right way. He taught me not to take for granted what I've been given. I honestly feel like I owe the world something for giving me such a talent and such an ability. I think I've been blessed by a lot and I've been given a lot. I'm just very grateful.

The one thing I don't like about my dad is that he always sets himself up to be ready for disappointment. He's a little bit more pessimistic than me—perhaps because a lot of disappointing things have happened in the past in his career. I always try to look for the positives in a given situation. I don't feel as snake-bitten as my dad's been and I just go with the flow.

Even now that I've signed my contract with the Timberwolves and I'm going to be a multimillionaire, the first words out of his mouth were, "Just remember that taxes take 50 percent of that. So don't spend your money frivolously!" That's pretty much the values he's instilled in me as a person. He's taught me to do the right things, save up for a rainy day, always study in school, and make sure that if basketball doesn't work out, I have something to fall back on. That pretty much typifies him.

Growing up, I always loved spending time with my dad. I loved going to his workouts and playing ball with him. And because we're so close, I always felt that we could discuss anything. I have friends, of course, from college and from the NBA. But my dad has always been my best friend.

◆ Wally Szczerbiak is a forward with the NBA's Minnesota Timberwolves. He was the sixth player chosen overall in the 1999 NBA draft.

(Photo courtesy of Walter Szczerbiak)

Wally Szczerbiak with his dad, Walter, and sister, Wendy (circa 1998).

Herman Cain

Chairman, Godfather's Pizza

MY FATHER WAS AN ENTREPRENEUR LONG BEFORE THE WORD BECAME POPULAR. We lived in Atlanta and Dad did whatever was necessary to make ends meet for my mom, my brother, and myself. That meant working three different jobs—as a barber, a janitor, and personal chauffeur and valet for Coca Cola CEO Robert Woodruff. Dad needed one job to put food on the table, one to put a roof over our heads, and one to save for the house he always dreamed of buying. (We lived in a duplex, which my brother and I referred to jokingly as "half a house.") Holding three jobs often meant working seven days a week, twenty hours a day. But I never once heard Dad complain or gripe.

It was amazing that he had any time for his family. But he always did. We attended church together every Sunday and he was always there to help with our homework. He was there, too, if we got into trouble at school. We respected Dad and he only had to tell us something once.

I remember a time in the seventh grade when Dad helped me get through a tough period. I was running for student body president and I thought I was going to win since I was a better student academically than my opponent. I had put up posters all over school, given speeches in the cafeteria at lunchtime, and probably talked to every student in every class at least three times. I worked harder for this than I ever had for anything else. When I lost it was a terrible disappointment. After a couple of days, Dad decided it was time for a talk.

We sat together at the kitchen table and Dad said, "Son, success is not measured by a single event. It is not something that can be achieved in one instant. It takes years of hard work to become successful and sometimes many attempts. And even then success is more about what is inside you than a list of accomplishments."

Dad lived this philosophy. Even though we didn't have much money, he was always willing to help others who were willing to help themselves.

He had no time for people who would depend totally on welfare. Dad believed that anything was possible for those who worked hard enough. I never heard him make excuses. My father was the hardest worker and most generous giver I have ever met.

When I was 13, Dad came home one summer day and told us we were going for a ride in the car. He drove to a suburb just west of the city and stopped in front of a six-room, red-brick house. "Welcome to our new home," Dad announced proudly. "We now have a whole house."

(Photo courtesy of Digital Restaurant Solutions Corporation)

Herman Cain

Luther Cain, Jr., my dad, is the first truly great man I ever knew. He lived his life so his family's could be better. He provided for us and he showed us love and affection. There are few more selfless acts. Dad died in 1982 but he will always be my hero.

◆ Herman Cain is the chairman of Godfather's Pizza.

Michael Weiss

Professional Figure Skater

My father has always been involved in athletics. He was on the 1964 U.S. Olympic gymnastics team, and today he owns two gyms. As a result, athletics has always been a part of my life.

I used to be a diver when I was younger, but one day I went to the rink with my dad and put on a pair of skates. I loved it and have been doing it ever since. I think the main reason that I've continued pushing myself is that my father has always had an enormous amount of confidence in me. Dad never complained when he had to take me to the rink at 6:00 in the morning. His number one priority has always been his kids.

In athletics, there are so many ups and downs and there are few people who are with you for the highs and the lows. That's why family is so important. It is really comforting for me to know that when I get off the ice, whether I skate my best program or my worst program, I am still going to get a hug from my family members. Just having that support means so much. My dad taught me that no matter what happens, my family is going to be there for me.

Dad also taught me to put my performances in the proper perspective. "Not every routine is going to be a 6.0," he often says. "What is important is not to get down on yourself. You should learn what you did wrong, and then go back and practice those things so the next time you compete, you don't make those same mistakes."

This attitude has instilled a great amount of confidence in me and everything I do. Dad taught me that if I make a decision that feels good deep down in my heart, then I am probably doing the right thing.

I never wanted my dad to feel like I disappointed him in some way. It's rare when it happens, but I can sure tell when he's disappointed! When I was 16 years old, my father bought a motorcycle. Initially, I started riding around with him on the back. But when I turned 17, I really wanted to start riding it myself. When I asked my dad, I didn't like his response.

"I don't want you to," he said. "You're too young and you have a lot ahead of you in terms of your skating career."

I knew my dad was right, but it didn't stop me from wanting to ride. Later that week, I took the test for motorcycle operators on one of my friend's motorcycles. When my dad saw me on my friend's bike, he said, "You can't go out and ride the motorcycle without a license."

I said, "Well, actually I have one."

Dad wasn't mad at me. He just shook his head and looked down. That was his way of letting me know that I didn't do the right thing.

One afternoon, I went out with my friends on our motorcycles and I got in an accident. Dad rushed home from work and when he came upstairs he said, "First and foremost, are you okay?

(Photo courtesy of Octagon Athlete Representation)

Michael Weiss with his dad, Greg.

I said, "Yeah, I'm fine."

I had a lot of gravel underneath my skin on my knee and shoulder, but other than that I was okay. But after seeing my dad's face that day, I swore off motorcycles forever!

My dad is particularly proud of my accomplishments. He's always bragging about me and telling people about the things that I have done. I think part of that pride comes from knowing that he had a direct influence on everything that I've achieved. My success proves that he did a terrific job raising me.

◈ Michael Weiss is the 2000 U.S. National Men's Figure Skating champion.

Jerry Greenfield

Co-founder, Ben & Jerry's

WHEN I WAS GROWING UP IN MERRICK, LONG ISLAND, IN THE 1960s, MY DAD WAS A stockbroker. Although that sounds like a pretty conservative job, my dad was definitely not an establishment type of person. In fact, my father has always been a real nonconformist who had a very healthy questioning of authority. That is something that he clearly communicated to me. I saw from an early age that my father was not affected by peer pressure. Our front lawn, for example, was not the model of beautiful lawn care! As the grass grew taller and taller and became browner and browner, all the neighbors used to try to subtly pressure him into upgrading his lawn care. But he'd say, "If they want to mow the lawn, they are free to go ahead and do just that." No one ever took him up on the offer!

One thing I remember very much about my father is that he was always involved in sports with me. My dad was very athletic and he passed his love of sports—particularly baseball—onto me. He was also very compassionate. I remember one time we were playing a little league game and we were beating the other team by quite a lot and it was just going on and on and on. Everyone on our team was getting a hit. As I was coming up to bat for the second time that inning, he told me to go up and strike out so that we would not continue the massacre of the other team. I did exactly as he instructed. I didn't even think of questioning my father. It wouldn't have occurred to me. He taught me that the idea is not to beat the other team into oblivion, but to just go out, play baseball, and have fun.

My father was more patient and less directive than I am. I think he believed in letting my brother, sister, and me figure things out for ourselves. I ended up going to college, which my parents were very supportive of. But my father always told me if I didn't want to go to college or if I wanted to collect trash for a living, that that was fine with him. He felt like the most important thing was for me to be happy and to find my way in life. For that reason, he was always extremely tolerant. Generally, I was a good kid. I didn't get into a lot of trouble, but I certainly had long hair! Dad thought I looked a little funny and a little weird-looking, but he was never put off or negative about it. He felt if this is a look I was comfortable with, that was good enough for him.

Dad used to talk to us all the time growing up about his experience in World War II, which I think for a lot of people of that generation was an incredibly formative event. He switched from being in the Army to the Air Corps because he didn't want to have to kill anyone. So Dad ended up getting a position where he was essentially flying people around in transport planes. That made a very big impression on me. In the late 1960s, I protested and marched to end the Vietnam War. Dad questioned authority and so did I.

When Ben Cohen and I decided to start a homemade ice cream parlor in Vermont, Dad was very surprised. I don't think he ever imagined either of us entering the business world. It wasn't like we opened a big business or anything. It was simply a homemade ice cream parlor that we renovated ourselves. Still, he got a kick out of the fact that we were business owners. I can still remember my parents coming up for the opening of the store. Dad and Mom pitched in all week scooping ice cream!

(Photo Credit: Gordon Miller. Courtesy of Ben & Jerry's.)

Jerry Greenfield with his dad, Malcolm.

Dad was very proud of what Ben and I accomplished. Since he had been working as a stockbroker all his life, he was very familiar with business and big companies. And he knew how corporate and impersonal they can be. But what Dad was most proud of was that we brought an element to our small ice cream parlor that he taught me—being human. I think that quality of being compassionate and considerate to others was actually very helpful in starting our little ice cream shop.

◆ Jerry Greenfield is the co-founder of Ben & Jerry's Ice Cream.

Jerry Brown

Mayor, Oakland, California

THE OBVIOUS LESSON I LEARNED FROM MY FATHER AT AN EARLY AGE WAS HOW to win elections. Beyond that, my father taught me about basic honesty. He had very high standards of ethics.

Dad made his initial mark in politics as the district attorney of San Francisco. He was not a strategist nor a tactician in a political sense. Rather, he was a person who believed government could do something and have a real, positive impact on people.

One case that tells a lot about who my father was dealt with a Mafia murder at a well-known bar in the North Beach section of the city. He was the lead prosecutor and he soon learned that his star witness was unreliable. My father never hesitated about what to do. He just walked into court and asked the judge to dismiss the case. It caused quite a stir in the city. He took a lot of criticism and he was ridiculed relentlessly by the papers. But I remember him telling me, "That's what you have to do in public service when you have been given a great deal of responsibility. You have to stand for principle." That incident demonstrated to me what a buoyant and resilient person my father was. He let that negative publicity roll off his back like water off a duck's back. He was very straightforward and a believer in the public interest. By today's standards, he was a very old-fashioned politician.

The yuppie, technocratic, poll-driven candidates are really a feature of the last 20 years. He was from an earlier period where candidates had to press the flesh, talk to people, and be accessible. I remember when I was in grammar school, our phone was actually listed in the phone book. And when it rang, I would often be told to get up from the dinner table and answer it. On the other end were just regular folks who wanted to talk to the district attorney about their problems. More often than not he got up and took the call. He was very intimately connected to peoples' concerns.

From the time my father was sworn in as district attorney in 1943, I learned the way of public life. Every night at the dinner table, he would talk about what's going on in the D.A.'s office. He believed that the main part of his job was to stand for what's right. I remember when he hired the first Chinese-American ever as the deputy district attorney in San Francisco. He also appointed the first African-American D.A., who later became a federal judge. He was a very inclusive politician who took a very socially conscious approach to public service.

My father also had a very good sense of humor. Because my

(Photo courtesy of Jerry Brown)

Jerry Brown with his dad, Pat.

father's father ran a little poker club and my mother's father was the police captain in charge of stopping gambling, he would often joke that one grandfather was going to end up arresting the other one! He was a wonderful storyteller and he had the remarkable gift of being able to make people feel at ease.

I was elected governor of California just eight years after he had left office. The day I was sworn was a very special day. He took a lot of pleasure in that, and I was extremely proud of what my father taught me.

◆ Jerry Brown is the mayor of Oakland, California. Like his father, he served as governor of California.

Brady Anderson

Center Fielder, Baltimore Orioles

MY MOM AND DAD DIVORCED WHEN I WAS THREE YEARS OLD. DESPITE THEIR breakup, I never felt neglected by either parent in any way. I spent my formative years living with my father in Burbank and San Diego, and he always went out of his way for me.

When I was seven, I loved to play ice hockey. But because hockey is not a very popular sport in Southern California, we had to play when the rinks weren't open to the public. This required my dad waking me up at midnight so that we could get to games by two in the morning. He did this on a regular basis and never complained. Later on, when I developed a love for baseball, my dad would take me to the batting cage and I would hit there for hours. It seemed like he would do anything for me.

Dad was always involved in my interests. He was my basketball and football coach until the ninth grade, and my baseball coach through my junior year of high school. My father was a great coach because he brought out the best in people. He could even get the worst players on the team to perform well. He did this by making it fun for them and making everyone want to play. You could almost see the relief on everyone's faces on the first day of practice when he announced that he wanted everyone to have fun.

My dad never preached to me. But I did have a few rules to follow, and telling the truth was the most important one. My dad taught me that even if I did something wrong, if I simply went to him and told the truth, the consequences of my actions would change. I may still get in trouble, but not nearly the trouble I would get into if I weren't honest with him. I learned that lesson at a very young age, so I was never tempted to lie to my father.

I also learned from my dad to always give my best effort in everything I do. Giving up or giving in a little bit has never really been an option for me. And it still isn't. That's why I don't get that upset after I have a particularly bad game. I may be a little disappointed, but I don't ever doubt my effort.

When I wasn't very highly recruited out of high school, my dad actually sent a clipping of me to the college baseball coach at UC-Irvine. I had a really good season my senior year in high school, but I truly believe that clipping helped me get into UCI. That was the break I needed and it led to a scholarship of $600.

My father was definitely a role model. His integrity is beyond reproach and he is incredibly genuine. He is the most solid man I have ever known.

It's also nice the way things worked out with my mom and dad. They are wonderful friends and never let their marital problems interfere with the way I was raised. As a result, not only do I love my mom and dad very much, but I'm also great friends with both of them.

(Photo courtesy of Professionals On Request, Ltd.)

Brady Anderson and his dad, Gerald.

◆ Brady Anderson is the all-star center fielder for the Baltimore Orioles.